Atget

the Pioneer

This book is published on the occasion of the exhibition
Eugène Atget, le pionnier
at the Hôtel de Sully, Paris,
June 23–September 17, 2000
and *Eugène Atget the Pioneer*
at the International Center of Photography, New York,
October 7, 2000 to January 21, 2001

The exhibition has been conceived and produced by the
Patrimoine photographique,
with the assistance of the
Ministère de la Culture et de la Communication
(Direction de l'Architecture et du Patrimoine).
Thanks are due to the
Bibliothèque nationale de France
and the
Banque de Neuflize, Schlumberger, Mallet, Demachy,
member of the ABN-AMRO group
for their exceptional assistance.

Exhibition curator
Jean-Claude Lemagny
in conjunction with Pierre Bonhomme

Technical curator in charge of coodination, works, and exhibition spaces
Yannick Vigouroux
with
Nicolas Desquinabo, Pascale Giffard and Marie Palleau
for the works
Stéphane Brochier, Jean-Philippe K-Bidi
for the exhibition spaces

text coordination
Philippe Cougrand

external relations
Noël Bourcier (design concept)
Olivier Bourgoin with Bérénice Robin (public relations)

publications
ElHabib Es Saadi

secretarial support
Martine Marques, Nadiège Paller

THANKS TO

Dieter Appelt
Sylvie Aubenas
Laure Beaumont-Maillet
Bernd & Hilla Becher
Hélène Darche, Jean Darche
Lee Friedlander
Bertrand-Pierre Galey
Dominica Kriz
Gilles Mora
Françoise Paviot

and to the following collectors, galleries, and institutions
Archiv Ann and Jürgen Wilde, Zülpich-Mülheim
August Sander Archiv, Cologne
Banque et Caisse d'Épargne de l'État, Luxemburg
Benjamin A. Hill, Decatur
Bibliothèque de l'Arsenal, Paris
Bibliothèque de l'École nationale des Beaux-Arts, Paris
Bibliothèque Doucet, Paris
Bibliothèque historique de la Ville de Paris
Bibliothèque nationale de France, Paris
Bill Brandt Archive LTD, London
Centre des Monuments nationaux, Paris
Fraenkel Gallery, San Francisco
Galerie Baudoin Lebon, Paris
George Eastman House, Rochester
The Historic New Orleans Collection
Maison européenne de la Photographie, Paris
Metropolitan Museum of Art, New York
Musée Carnavalet, Paris
Musée de l'Île-de-France, Sceaux
Musée des Arts décoratifs, Paris
Musée national d'Art moderne, Centre Georges Pompidou, Paris
Museum of Modern Art, New York
Philadelphia Museum of Art
Sandra Alvarez de Toledo, Paris
as well as to those lenders who prefer to remain anonymous

Jean-Claude Lemagny

Atget
the Pioneer

Sylvie Aubenas
Pierre Borhan
Luce Lebart

Prestel
Munich · London · New York

Atget, The Posthumous Pioneer

When, in 1926, Man Ray offered to publish some of Atget's photographs in numbers 7 and 8 of *La Révolution surréaliste*, Atget begged him not to mention his name. He was obviously of the opinion that he could have nothing to do with a group of avant-garde artists who — sometimes playfully and ironically, at other times in all seriousness and even pomposity — were creating such a stir in the worlds of thought, art, and social life. Man Ray — who lived at 31 Rue Campagne-Première, whereas Atget himself was at number 17 *bis* — had already purchased around 50 prints from the photographer. Atget however could scarcely have countenanced the fact that Man Ray's offer was to constitute an initial step in a recognition that the by now elderly man could no longer have hoped for. It is true that several of his views of Paris had already appeared in Charles Simon's *Paris de 1800 à 1900* and in *Paris* by Georges Riat, but he remained a solitary figure, independent and ignored by the press. No one had distracted him from his path, neither the late-nineteenth-century Pictorialists, nor twentieth-century enthusiasts whose every effort was directed towards ushering in the modern age. The portrait that Berenice Abbott (at the time Man Ray's assistant) took of him in 1927 a few days prior to his death was not in fact a sign of his nascent fame, but a gesture of sympathy on the part of a youthful admirer who had only recently opened a studio of her own. It would be these two Americans, however, who would allow Atget to break free from his milieu and from the near anonymity which had been his lot since he had started out in photography. So it is that the destiny of works of art can be at least as extraordinary as that of men.

Jean Eugène Auguste Atget was born February 12, 1857 in Libourne, near Bordeaux. Orphaned as a child, he was brought up by his maternal grandparents and his uncle, and was taught Greek and Latin. At first he wanted to become an actor and followed Edmond Got's course at the National Conservatoire of the Dramatic Arts. For the following 15 or so years, he was attached to various groups of repertory players; appearing on the stage often without ever taking a leading role. His lifelong companion, Valentine Compagnon, whom he met around 1886, encountered greater success — unspectacular perhaps, but noteworthy — yet Atget was always passed over. When finally he had to decide on another career, he turned at first to painting. Lacking any great talent, he nonetheless discovered that his colleagues often needed documents of all kinds, and so he shifted to photography, choosing to work for illustrators, decorative artists, architects, publishers, and lovers of "old Paris" as well as for painters. He sold his prints to Utrillo, Vlaminck, and Dunoyer de Segonzac, to Derain, Kisling, and Foujita as well as to the Musée Carnavalet, the Bibliothèque Historique of the City of Paris, and the Bibliothèque Nationale. If he cannot be said to have taken up photography as a vocation, he was to pursue it conscientiously nonetheless for over three decades.

It seems that he did not socialize with other photographers of his time. His death, on August 4, 1927, went largely unremarked and scarcely anyone accompanied his body to the cemetery at Bagneux. His work, however — comprising just under 10,000 prints — did not fall into oblivion. Though the man himself had no children, the photographer was to beget a varied family of followers, some of them masters in their own right. Possessed of an entirely utilitarian approach to the medium, Atget never went in for "art for art's sake." His posthumous fame has nonetheless made him — as André Jammes remarked at the 1985 Atget Symposium organized at the Collège de France in Paris — into one of the "Fathers of the Church" of photography. Emmanuel Sougez put it succinctly: "Atget never realized that he was Atget." Just as, for 60 years, Jacques-Henri Lartigue had no real grasp of what he had achieved in photography, Atget too misjudged his life's work. It was painting that was to count the most for Lartigue, but it was the stage that was to hold Atget in thrall. As a supplier of "documents for artists," he displayed all the scrupulousness of a professional who strives to do the best job he can, but he never saw himself as an artist. An individualist, he placed little store by the opinions of others and worked hard at his topographic surveys with no thought of competing alongside the public's favorite sons. Gifted with uncompromising intelligence as well as with a visual receptiveness that he made no attempt to compare with that of others, he was at once noble in the moral sense yet artistically humble. He was a marginal figure because he never associated with any coterie (not even a photographic club) but even more because the demands he made on himself were entirely of his own devising, rather than being borrowed from some prior intellectual authority. Atget — the historian of urbanism, the observer of the decorative arts as applied to architecture, the archivist, collector, "author/publisher," and poet — resists all attempts at being pigeonholed since not only is his work multifarious but his modernity is bound up with a tradition that he respects.

It took others — in particular Charles Rado and John Szarkowski — to recognize the photographic talent of Lartigue who had been blinkered by his attachment to painting. In the same way, though it was Atget himself who had sensed an unspoken enchantment behind the real world, he never thought of himself as a magician, and only Man Ray and Berenice Abbott were able to gauge his true worth.

Through the good offices of "Atget's oldest and closest friend," André Calmettes, who had been entrusted with the disposal of the photographer's estate, Berenice Abbott purchased the remaining glass-plates and prints in June 1928 and shipped them to New York. She exhibited this collection as well as she could, publicizing it in various articles. Invited to participate in the "Film und Foto" exhibition held in Stuttgart in 1929, she showed Atget's photographs in conjunction with her own. Back in the United States the same year, Abbott published an article on Atget in *Creative Art*.[1] Short of funds, she disposed of 50 per cent of the rights to her Atget collection to Julien Levy for $1,000, and assisted the gallery owner in making her idol more widely known to a New York audience. She was the driving-force behind the first book ever devoted to Atget, published in 1930, *Atget, photographe de Paris* — the French edition had a preface by the celebrated novelist Pierre Mac Orlan — which benefited from an international readership since it came out in German and American editions the same year. It is without doubt to Abbott, whose discernment was equaled only by her dogged determination, that Atget could be said to owe the lion's share of his posthumous fame. She was to sell her collection of work by the man she described as a "mutant of his time"[2] to the Museum of Modern Art in 1968, entrusting it to the museum's conservator of photography and so passing on Atget's flame. It is uncertain, however, who of Berenice Abbott or Man Ray had initiated Atget's participation in 1928 at the first Independent Salon of Photography — the "Salon de l'Escalier" — at the Comédie des Champs-Élysées, at which another great, late artist, Nadar, also participated, joined by André Kertész, Germaine Krull, Paul Outerbridge, and other young talents of a similar caliber. Atget's name was misspelt in the catalogue (where it came out as "Adget") as well as by a number of commentators, though such oversights did not prevent the critic of the *Chicago Tribune* from seeing this elder as a pioneer. From this point, illustrations of his work appeared and the articles flowed, the most notable being by the editor of *L'art vivant* Florent Fels, Surrealist poet Robert Desnos, and contemporary art critic Waldemar George. In May 1929, photographs by Atget adorned the cover of an issue of *Le Crapouillot* devoted to Paris, while in 1931, Walter Benjamin included Atget in his *Small History of Photography*. In an article in a 1937 issue of *Vogue*, M. F. Agha summed up the situation perfectly, observing that the Moderns had elevated Atget into a "Saint and Martyr of modern photography."

The appreciative reactions to Atget on the part of photographers, the lessons they could draw from him, and the ways they extended his work were of still greater significance. Walker Evans first encountered prints by Atget at Berenice Abbott's in November 1929. Finding himself presented with "such magnificent strength and style" and taking a liking to Atget's "lyrical understanding of the street" he soon went on to write a laudatory piece on him for *Hound and Horn*[3] a couple of years later. Like Atget himself, Evans was capable of zeroing in on what was important to him in the real world and of capturing it in a photograph. Edward Weston, perusing the newly published book sent him by Jean Charlot, made a number of observations on Atget's work in his *Daybooks* dated December 27, 1930. As for Ansel Adams, he voiced his opinion in *The Fortnightly* of November 6, 1931. Still in the United States, it is unarguable that Lee Friedlander was later to learn greatly from Atget's example, in evidence as much in his *Flowers and Trees* as in *The American Monument*, where he eschewed the kind of patriotic overkill that it is difficult to resist in such subject matter, and that Atget, years before, had entirely banished from his views of Paris and its surroundings. Either directly, or else via Evans and Friedlander, other American photographers began to detect pointers or echoes in the work of Atget, though at this stage we prefer to focus on the dialogue between different works since it is beyond our scope to draw up an exhaustive list of his influence or even of his followers.

In Germany it was Atget's objectivity — his capacity to make "objective statements" — and the way he would compose series (door-knockers, store signs, entrance grills, banister rails, etc.) that found echoes in the work of another analyst and organizer of forms, Albert Renger-Patzsch, as well as among other proponents of New Objectivity all the way down to Bernd and Hilla Becher. Were not the latter also swayed by Atget's working methods, by his approach to subjects and his framing of them? Walter Benjamin relished the fact that Atget "was the first to disinfect the atmosphere," to "cleanse" and "wash" it.[4] For their part, the Bechers, who transformed industrial buildings into historical monuments, appreciated the photographer—archeologist's gift for concentrating on his subject alone. Nothing more, nothing less. Theirs is a typological program of a retrospective nature which offers conclusive evidence that the German offshoot of Atget's posterity is not the least important.

The Czech Surrealist painter Jindřich Štyrský discovered Atget's work during a stay in Paris from 1925 to 1928. In 1934 and 1935, Štyrský himself completed three series or cycles of photographs, the last of which, *Après-midi à Paris*, was still more redolent of the earlier photographer

[1] "Eugène Atget by Berenice Abbott", *Creative Art*, volume 5, no. 3, September 1929, pp. 651–56. [2] Berenice Abbott, *The World of Atget*, Berkeley Publishing Corporation, 1977, p. XXI. [3] Quoted from Belinda Rathbone, *Walker Evans: A Biography*, London: Thames and Hudson, 1995, p. 69; see Walker Evans, "The Reappearance of Photography," *Hound and Horn*, October—December 1931, pp. 125–28. [4] Walter Benjamin, "A Small History of Photography" in *One-Way*

of stalls, store windows and fences, of fairgrounds and mannequins, since — betraying a kindred spirit — Štyrský compiled it in the great city of visual poetry. As early as the 1930s Atget's universal appeal was assured.

In France, photographers such as Marcel Bovis and Robert Doisneau were moved above all by some of the populist subjects to which Atget had been receptive: tradesmen and small shopkeepers, street life and public entertainments, which he captured with an old, 18x24-centimeter view bellows camera and Lumière plates. Others, from René-Jacques to Bruno Réquillart, were more in tune with his feeling for perspective, his approach to space, and his composition of the image. If, as a student of Man Ray's, Bill Brandt had "loved the poetry of his street scenes, the beggars, the prostitutes, the musicians" that inhabit Atget's world, he was equally "enchanted by the steep perspective of his cobblestone streets,"[5] the Englishman's enchantment translating into some of his own landscapes. One relishes too the reminiscences of Atget in the magnificently composed shots of the gardens at Versailles taken by Bruno Réquillart in 1977. Between the 1930s and 1960s, there was little research and only a few studies and critical pieces on Atget, notable exceptions being those by Ferdinand Reyher (made public in part on the occasion of the exhibition mounted in 1948 at the Addison Gallery of American Art), Yvan Christ, author of *Saint-Germain-des-Prés 1900, vu par Atget* which appeared in 1951, and Minor White, whose studies were published in *Image* in April 1956. When the faithfully devoted Berenice Abbott brought out the first edition of *The World of Atget* in 1964, analysis started up again on both sides of the Atlantic. Jean Leroy, Leslie Katz, Clement Greenberg, John Fraser, Romeo Martinez, Alain Pougetoux, and others partially lifted the veil over the photographer's life and personality. Atget's persona was becoming clearer: he was a secretive man, ill at ease with informality and the outpourings of the soul, more interested in politics and history than in everyday events. He was also a self-taught photographer, methodical, driven by an inner conviction, unwavering in his choice of equipment and processes. Confident of the subject matter he chose, he was antagonistic to the idea of portraiture and did not even take those of Valentine Compagnon, of André Calmettes, or of any of the painters he visited. He remained more in touch with the places and objects he shot (and thus could save from oblivion) than with recreating the atmosphere typified by social interactions and in human activities, as if the world and the men in it were not made for each other. A non-conformist who turned a blind eye to the Belle Époque and an anti-militarist who took as little part as possible in World War I, his photographs of Paris show scant interest in Haussmann's new city, though in reality it affected his work, rendering him unable to complete his book on art in the old quarters. A much appreciated forerunner, he has been venerated by fellow-artists as diverse as Manuel Alvarez-Bravo, Vilem Kriz, Clarence John Laughlin, Walker Evans, Bill Brandt, Lee Friedlander, and Michael Kenna. Though his commentators consider him unclassifiable, Atget is acknowledged by most as the uncompromising advocate of descriptive photography, whether it stays on the surface of things or strives to go deeper.

It was John Szarkowski and Maria Morris Hambourg who elevated Atget to the canon with a four-volume work published between 1981 and 1985, *The Work of Atget*. Essential reading, these tomes give one the opportunity to appreciate without bias both the photographer of tradition who was fond of "roots" (both literal and figurative) and who performed the work of memory, and the more rebellious figure, who blazed a new trail — albeit unknowingly. They were thus the first to situate the work — free of all compromise — in the context of its overall posterity.

The colloquium organized in 1985 at the Collège de France under the aegis of Pierre Barbin and Jean-François Chevrier, as well as the special issue of the journal *Photographies* that followed, combined forces to secure acceptance forever of Atget's multifarious contribution to the history of photography. In the Musée Carnavalet, Françoise Reynaud made better known a number of aspects of his work and, together with David Harris, cast some light on the working methods of the by now mythical craftsman. In Michel Frizot's *New History of Photography* (first published in French in 1994), Atget is the only photographer to be allotted a whole chapter of his own (written by Molly Nesbit).

The very diversity of Atget's admirers, be they photographers, historians, or conservators, is a reflection of one of the characteristics of his work which, by dint of its axiomatic ambiguity and in spite of its coherence, escapes every attempt to pin it down. In the year 2000, Atget's work still remains a treasure trove for images of the remnants of Old Paris as it was in 1900. Jean-Claude Lemagny, however, also delights in the door it opens on to a dreamworld: "Atget's genius," he wrote, "resides in the fact that he is a master of the realm of dreams."[6] One and the same picture can fulfill a utilitarian function: as a fragment of knowledge from which "*père* Atget" has withdrawn entirely, but it can also find its place and radiate out from the more glorious sphere of pure art, where freedom to interpret is essentially unlimited. Atget was also a pioneer for both Walter Benjamin, who saw his pictures as "the scene of a crime," and for Waldemar George, who felt that they hailed the "advent of the object." Capable of the plainest as well as the most insightful views, he sold them all at the same price, providing no keys with which to read his work. Atget was a man rooted in the past in terms of equipment, technique, and choice of subject, yet he was also a photographer of his time in his preoccupation with documents, and a timeless artist in his analysis of form as well as in that mastery of both the frontal view and the perspectival vista that makes his work such a delight. When he is at the summit of his art, his vision is concise, his views impeccably structured, yet at the same time he gives free rein to an imagination that remains firmly anchored in the real. Space can be cleansed, but this does not prevent its being spiritualized, though

Street and Other Writings, London: Verso, 1979 (repr.2000), pp. 249–50   [5] Letter of April 8, 1978 to Maria Morris Hambourg, Atget Archives, MoMA, New York.
[6] Jean-Claude Lemagny, "La matière, l'ombre et la fiction," in *La Recherche photographique*, 4, May 1988, p. 41.   [7] Leslie Katz, "An Interview with Walker Evans" [1971], in *Photography in Print: Writings from 1816 to the Present* (ed. Vicki Goldberg), New York: Simon and Schuster, 1981, p. 366.

without exaggeration. This escape from the theatrical threw off melancholia by transforming the whole world into a special kind of photograph, which, shot through with integrity and purity, constantly renews itself through the *ars magna* of representation. Walker Evans wrote of Atget that "he could infuse the street with his own poetry."[7] Atget became an inspiration to photographers of every stamp, emboldening their own projects and offering clarity to their visions. However different his successors were, Atget's creativity fertilized the soil for countless works to come, permeating and enriching them.

Every artist's oeuvre lies somewhere on a long line of things given and things borrowed: every work is in some way transitional. It will nourish knowledge, even when one cannot point to the precise nature of its contribution. Among all the transformations that have affected the history of photography, Atget's creative oeuvre marks the onset of some of its most significant developments — amounting to consecrations.

PIERRE BORHAN

Atget the Prophet

There stands at the very heart of the history of photography an exceptional if strange figure: Eugène Atget. His oeuvre has left its mark through its sheer size, as well as through the serene beauty it exudes. Yet, in spite of all the efforts of photography historians, intending to forge the links between successive artists and their styles into a causal chain following the model of the history of painting, Atget's work stands alone, shrouded in the unbroken silence of its creator. Atget's immense influence has exerted itself through what others have seen in it and not through what they have written. We shall show here how, though his path was an arduous one, it became a rich source for others and that he proved to be an ever more commanding presence right up to today and will continue to be so into the future.

Atget, who was an actor for many years, was well aware of the power of words. He read voraciously, all Victor Hugo's works, for example. He knew better than most the evocative potential of the images contained in a text. He expressed his literary and artistic opinions forcefully and would buttonhole his neighbors with interminable booming diatribes: "Eat your fill, Sirs! Oh Ministers, full of integrity...." And, under the aegis of a then vibrant popular culture (now long defunct), he would give lectures and public readings. Yet on photography, nothing. "Documents for artists," read his advertisement, implying: "I am *not* the artist." Documents, then, for others to use.

Humble, self-effacing in his social relations, Atget was a man rooted in the past. Man Ray — a great admirer of his — found Atget's appearance rather nondescript. Perhaps the youthful American did not understand that he was in the presence of a representative of the Old France, from a time when the subtlest form of politeness was unaffectedness. It is easy to imagine, too, that Atget was sufficiently attentive to refined language not to want to soil it with the kind of cant that arises from untimely conflict between words and forms, and that he felt too much respect for his work to want to shore it up with explanations. He knew that those who really know how to look scarcely feel the need to say anything.

The value of a work of art stands in inverse proportion to the number of ideas that can be attached to it. To grasp this simple truth, however, one must first dispel a number of illusions. At first glance, the most admired works are also those which can be analyzed in the most diverse ways. Convinced that this is indeed the case, some have tried to beguile us by ingeniously concocting artworks which by their very esotericism necessitate myriad commentaries. This has occurred, for example, with a great number of mediocre Surrealist paintings. The supreme illustration of this — though on a higher aesthetic plane — is Marcel Duchamp's *The Large Glass* which attempted to invert the age-old hierarchy between artwork and discourse by disposing the viewer to drown the former (which alludes to the immaterial through its very transparency) in the latter (furthered by the pseudo-scientific appearance of its design). In this way, in a world crushed by technology and much more concerned with abstract connections than by the apparition of being, the dominance of speech is once more vindicated. Yet Duchamp actually achieved the opposite result. In spite of all the commentaries in which he was forced to indulge to make his experiment work, in the end *The Large Glass* points to the inanity of words and appears as it is, unapproachable and silent, at rest within itself through the visual power of the forms it materializes.

"Documents for artists." Any document derives its value solely from discourse. But a document is not in itself a discourse. It hovers in strict conceptual neutrality, indifferently open to the interpretations of those who put it to use. It neither puts itself forward, nor alludes. For a historian, the selective commentaries of another historian are less a "document" than a legally binding contract. They can only be turned into "documents" by a further operation, when the personal intentions of the writer are bracketed off, and they are returned to the status of being freely interpretable.

A "document" is not wholly incompatible with a "work of art," however. The document does not take sides, it awaits an interpretation, often by knowledge, though on occasion by reason or sensitivity too. A document marks the emersion of a single reality from among all other realities. Unless one believes in a *deus ex machina* manipulating everything from behind the scenes, a document offers itself up as a presence that is all the fuller, all the weightier, and all the more complete as it is as yet unsullied by any interference from interpretation. "I make documents," is what Atget said — and we are now entitled to add, "and so I can also make works of art, since you are free to see in them what you will." Art always leads us back to this original state of freedom. The only concept for which there is room is that of being able to act therein with no prior models: the concept then which states that, on the threshold of art, concepts themselves have no currency, since, from here on, sensitivity can blossom in every direction.

For some time the project that Atget had fixed so very clearly in his mind has given the impression that his career was only loosely connected to photographic history, as it is customarily recorded. Was Atget unaware of the artistic pretensions of some types of photography of his time: the Salons or the celebrated Pictorialists? It is unlikely that he had never heard speak of them, but he certainly felt that they were no concern of his. He shut himself up completely within his role as a documentary photographer. As far as we know, he never took a close-up portrait nor even still lifes in the traditional artistic sense, manifesting a total absence of ambition, even perhaps of interest, in that direction.

Quite unlike Alfred Stieglitz or Pierre Dubreuil, who became conscious of the development of the art of photography and who at the same time gave it fresh impetus, Atget, in these terms, only counts because of the vastness of his oeuvre and by the impassioned way in which young artists and poets have looked at it. Though Atget's aesthetic influence was formidable and even meteoric, he felt no real need of it, and towards the end of his life he even rejected it.

Such a paradoxical situation — one with no conscious antecedents (not even Marville) and no acknowledged descendants — seems to us to provide a prime illustration of the distinction between the history of art and an Imaginary Museum. The Imaginary Museum is an intellectual space in which the most diverse aesthetic judgments are to be allowed free rein. The specific features of each piece, however, draw dividing lines between each work of art that have nothing to do with distinctions of history and geography. An Imaginary Museum is anything but eclectic.

The Imaginary Museum is ranged against the history of art. The latter is an accumulation of data — it thus belongs to the universe of knowledge. The Imaginary Museum is a group of artworks, however diverse they may be, that offer a foothold for the judgments of our sensibility. It belongs to the world of feeling, to aesthetics in the etymological sense of the word. The history of art is dominated by relationships that explain things through cause and effect, since history is obliged to describe and to interpret. The Imaginary Museum is ruled by comparisons in value and eschews determinism, since each work of art brings with it a new quality into the world.

In art history, the place and date of birth of each artwork is a basic given that allows the direction of causal explanations to be established. Topographic and chronological considerations cannot be separated from others — psychological ones, or political, economic, and sociological ones — that ensnare the works in a web of connections derived from areas beyond the immediate sphere of art. In an effort to explain art, one must look beyond it, examining the external influences, before returning to focus on the artwork in question.

In the Imaginary Museum, within the aesthetic field, the notions and antinomies that are applicable and which operate elsewhere meld or else dissolve. Objective and subjective, for example, are no longer opposites, but instead reinforce each other. The same is true of form and content, since henceforth content itself becomes form. The categories of the useful and the useless too are both subsumed beneath a usefulness that underpins their very existence. Face-to-face encounters replace communication: it is a world where meaning has no place, where meaning vanishes and leaves the coast clear for the advent of the pure materiality of artworks that are sufficient *in* themselves but which can now enter into comparisons and engage in a dialogue that owes nothing to historical circumstances. In this world, the essential movement is not one from the past to the future, as it is in history; it is a world of an unending return to the origin.

In the Imaginary Museum, all the encounters, all the harmonies, and confrontations occur between the forms themselves as they arise from an art *qua* aesthetic reality, indifferent to all other considerations. To speak of art is to enter into an arena of thought quite independent from any other. As Heidegger has reminded us: the origin of the work of art lies in art and vice versa, and this circle has to be accepted as a "joy of thought" that enables one to disclose oneself to the residuum of things. The awareness of the existence of the Imaginary Museum unpacks art historical hierarchies, however diverse these may appear. The Imaginary Museum has no truck with different levels of civilization, nor with the political will, nor with individual psychology, nor with economic power. The connection that was thought incontrovertible between historical structure and cultural achievement is completely surpassed. Artworks conflict or agree with each other simply through their visual — or their auditory — realities. Through the work, art engages with the very status of receptivity in human thought.

The fact that Atget's self-reliant, stormy, almost libertarian spirit had partially cut him off from the well-trodden paths of the history of photography meant that he was ideally suited to the admiration of innovative minds. If its position in the rollcall of schools and styles is uneasy, his work finds a commanding place at the very heart of the Imaginary Museum of world photography. Simultaneously, Atget's oeuvre has helped photography itself earn acceptance within the universal Imaginary Museum of art. After primitive art, child art, and the art of the insane, it was only right and proper that photography too should join the all-embracing orbit of the Imaginary Museum, though the importance accorded hand-crafting long mitigated against its recognition as a legitimate art form. For that to happen, there had first to emerge a whole new concept in art — or rather the end point of any aesthetic thought — the ready-made. A ready-made is an object that becomes an artwork simply by being designated as such and whose new-found nature is brought out by displacing it from its customary setting. The photographer too does not disturb the object at which he points his camera; he contents himself merely by making his images permanently transportable. Of course, a photograph is not an unaided ready-made since the photographer, when he takes the picture, selects one out of all the possible angles and lighting conditions, but often his intention is — as far as it is possible — to let the complete object come forth, to present it to another exactly as it appears to his own eyes. This is very much Atget's way: whatever is chosen remains just as it was when chosen.

But who chose it? When Duchamp was asked: "How do you choose your ready-mades?" he replied: "They do the choosing." A profound quip that belies Duchamp the intellectual joker and restores him to the position of every artist, of one who feels chosen to return to a primal sense of wonder and to allow us all to experience it once again.

The events Atget photographed during his peregrinations can be imagined as one vast collection of ready-mades. Since Duchamp has taught us that the notion of a work of art can be extended indefinitely and all one needs are fresh eyes, Atget's painstaking project, which was long thought to be the epitome of the naive artist, instead seems today a supreme example of a pure and liberated artistic process. Thus, in a way that we are still trying to come to grips with, a photographer — received into the artistic community at the very end of his life by the Surrealists, thanks to the dreamlike resonance of some his images — already stood at the heart of Duchamp's conception of an art restored to its innate capacity to surprise.

Denis Roche has written about the vertigo experienced by an owner of a camera who cannot stop taking pictures of everything and anything. Such vertigo is not naivete, rather an innate characteristic of any human being who senses the need to produce a double of the world and thus assure himself that he does indeed exist. Unchaneled, this dizziness might have amounted to lunacy, but Atget the creator was able to impart structure and limits to it, while preserving its character as an endless visionary journey. With Atget, formal beauty is not only to be found within the composition of the image, but spreads to his entire tireless but ordered quest.

As one peruses all the thousands of prints located in Parisian collections, there emanates a sensation of monotony which seems at odds with creative inventiveness. These worthy efforts of a camera-wielding journeyman, who strove to fill every last gap in his archive, place Atget at some remove from the customary idea of an artist as a man who selects his motifs subjectively and who can rise above the constraints of his immediate environment. On occasion, we even doubt our own judgment. Presented with such a prosaic, such a repetitive record, we too start to feel misgivings. More precisely, the mind is split into two contrasting attitudes. Some images are indeed exceptional, that much is obvious: but, after all, is not photography the only art able to throw up masterpieces by accident? And

then perhaps the rest results from obeying the time-honored dictates of historical architecture. Sometimes the eyes glaze over and we experience a kind of numbness. But another, frequent way of looking, at once more invigorating and more gratifying, is much to be preferred; it sees something marvelous in every one of Atget's photographs. (We will return below to a number of prime cases of this, such as the door-knocker series.) Drably documentary images are few and far between, however; there emerges most of the time an image of space, a presence which remains ineffable (this last is a word scoffed at by idiots, though it provides a starting-point for any true critical meditation). From within the expanse of the image there emerges, on the one hand, an architectural, volumetric, and plastic solidity, and, on the other, the atmosphere of place and its singular spirit. In Atget, these are reconciled, so resolving — and on the very highest level — the contradictory qualities that all the best photographs generally share.

As for the door-knocker series, if looked at attentively it brings us into contact with a modernity that it is nothing short of contemporary. Let us posit an exhibition hung in two different ways. The first would comprise vast alignments of Atget's door-knockers, all facing us darkly, each framed in exactly the same way. An attempt, then, to force the visitor to go through the doors of boredom, and experience for himself the fact that no two door-knockers are completely alike (and this is precisely what Atget had in mind), to show that sheer persistence can open up a new world. At the end of these remorseless rows of photographs, themselves transformed into potent denizens of the exhibition space, are several works by Bernd and Hilla Becher. With their imperturbable arrays of almost identical industrial buildings, the Bechers have already shown that a documentary approach, divorced from any "aesthetic" effect (in inverted commas, since, if the word has any meaning at all, such matters will always boil down to questions of aesthetics), could turn back on itself and metamorphose into a work of art. It remains a moot point whether such a specific presentation would indeed be feasible; it would amount more to an installation than an exhibition.

The other possible project — similarly inspired by the Bechers' work — involves hanging various sequences of views by Atget that were especially, though never entirely, repetitive. They would be hung in geometric panels with frames one on top of the other, the end result being to cover the walls with highly significant forms that could be read on two levels: as abstract pattern and as multiple variations. Here, however, the Bechers' example is no longer valid and it would have been tantamount to a betrayal of Atget's works. Placed in rows, they make it possible to compare objects that are at once similar and different. Aligned and stacked one on top of the other, however, the invasive, geometric way they are presented deprives us of their one-off, solitary quality. The tension between this process of enumeration and typology, which has since become a possible indicator of art and the search for the "uncanny" quality that attaches itself to a particular place — an ahistorical procedure if ever there was one — is one of the major strengths of Atget's oeuvre.

Today it seems as if Atget's painstaking, unrelenting quest, as he crisscrossed the streets of Paris bent beneath a massive box and tripod, no longer runs counter to the idea we have of the pure artist. For even that was art. Far removed from the worldly platitudes espoused by doctrines of the "when attitudes become works of art" school, Atget's example shows how a photographer, braving hard work, exhaustion, and incomprehension, managed to transform the processes inherent in the exercise of a certain type of photography into the construction of a complete form of life that is (just like an artwork) adopted and controlled, and which thus must live within and through silence.

We are always coming across sudden accelerations in Atget's career that set him apart from traditional history. By not participating in mainstream photographic history, he lies beyond our timelines and is left to circulate freely among the different artistic values of the Imaginary Museum, as he points both back into the past and forwards into the future. For Atget — an artist whose modernity we have been striving here to bring out — was also a man with deep roots in the past. This is true even in his most boldly individual images and with respect not only to style and subject, but also to technique, as with his outdated camera and in the dark-hued foliations that transport us back to the time before panchromatic emulsion. Though he explored every nook and cranny of Paris, in an implicit protest against the all-pervasive presence of modern vulgarity, he never once photographed the Eiffel Tower. He set out to document horse-drawn vehicles at the very time they started vanishing from the streets. Paris in the 1920s was already packed with automobiles, but Atget scarcely registered their existence, and when they do appear it is as bizarre, gleaming objects, alone and out of place in some age-old courtyard in *vieux* Paris: Atget might have been co-opted by the Cubists, by the Surrealists, and even by Conceptual artists — but certainly not by the Futurists.

In his images of the Paris hinterland, it is not the mushrooming horror of the suburbs that comes to the fore, but the little old hamlets — albeit perhaps only temporarily preserved. They are so pretty, so joyous, that we feel in the presence of a kind of vision, one that not even Atget could ever have seen with his own eyes; vistas, which like the memory of some past life, open "onto some marvelous apparition, far off in the silence and in the purity of all that lies in the thrall of death" (Holger Trülzsch).

This world, in which time has gone into reverse, is split into two main realms. First, there is Old Paris, steeped in the desires of men and in chance encounters, a great heap, and so immeasurably diverse as to become uniform. Secondly, there are the great parks created by royal edict, frozen instants of the undivided sovereign will, laid out according to the rules of classical perspective. Turning a corner and entering some ancient courtyard, Atget could always come across a new detail with which to enrich an already vast collection. At

Versailles or at Saint-Cloud, however, he had to operate within a pre-existent masterpiece in which everything had already been measured and calculated. In those gardens, Atget learnt that there is no such thing as an innocent point of view, that one's gaze as one walks round is at every turn selecting from among the rigor a composition which at that moment could be the work of no one else. On one side, then, Atget moves through Old Paris making discoveries and lists, as through an homogenous substance. On the other, he understood that the form of an image emerges at first from within, from a construction that has to be built up afresh each time. Through this dual experience and in a most intimate way, Atget lived and felt the two poles of the artistic process — encounter and mastery — and delved deep within them both.

As he walked through the capital, this "Piéton de Paris" was prey to two types of emotion: the first was a sense of poetry deriving from its tragic history; the other stemmed from the bizarre imaginings of a wandering bard. On the one side, Hugo's *Les Misérables;* on the other, Gérard de Nerval's *Aurélia*. For these harmless-looking streets witnessed all the atrocities of civil war. To the right, the Rue Transnonain, on the left the cloister at Saint-Merry. There have been shootings everywhere, be it during the royalist insurrection of Vendémiaire, in the Revolution of June 1848, or under the Commune. Old Paris is a battlefield, and such sinister memories can readily ooze from its blackened walls or from its shadowy doorways.

At the same time though, Paris provides the perfect backdrop for many a blissful family existence and is ideally suited to the enjoyment of the good things in life. The Cour de Rohan, the Rue Saint-André-des-Arts, the *quais* of the Seine lined with the *bouquinistes'* bookstalls, the quiet easefulness of antique things worn smooth by habit is tirelessly evoked by certain images. This is its picturesque side. Neither of these two aspects interested Atget. He seized the present as it appeared, prior to any cultural preconceptions. The intense poetry emanating from his work spurns the hackneyed collusion between literature and sentimentality: it transpires instead from the simple fact that things exist. In his professional life, Atget had placed himself at the disposal of others, bowing to the interpretations of those who use his pictures, and yet his extreme sensitivity to space and his consummate compositional skill imbue each image with an inimitable stamp. The intersection of these two tendencies disclose a personality: but can Atget be said to possess a "style"?

To speak of style in connection with Atget perhaps amounts to a malapropism. It is often the case that the greatest masterpieces have nothing to do with style. To have "a style" presupposes some supplementary formal gesture such as having curlicues, having an accent or mark that can be as easily recognized as a fragrance. Atget's photographs hover midway between the spurning of all romantic dramatization of space and an unawareness of the possible modernist abandonment of resemblance. If Marville invested Haussmann's disemboweling of Paris with epic scope, Atget could see nothing of worth in the ruins he stumbled across. He remained powerless, swaying, dismayed in the face of such waste and confusion. Walker Evans would have made something of this blackened mess of beams, but just this once Atget abandoned art for moralizing and expressed his disapproval of the carnage by holding his talent in check. What affected him was the way life carried on regardless among these old things, represented by such objects as a well, a trellis, or a porch. His work ushers his viewers into a shared realm. For Atget, as for the majority of his contemporaries, it was obvious that to achieve this the viewer must first be made to grasp what exactly the realm was. It is well documented that Atget would often return to a place years after first recording it, to photograph it once again and more closely, but he ignored the fact that one can detach oneself from representation to delve deep into the precise structure of things. He apparently left such boldness to the initiative of his clients, the "artists," though at the period concerned it is improbable that many availed themselves of the opportunity.

Neither the grand gestures opening into infinity of a Gustave Le Gray marine picture (from 1856), nor the discoveries of Paul Strand in 1916, for whom objects can be presented without a linguistic intermediary (a process foolishly termed "abstract"), have much common ground with Atget, whose work is suspended between these two extremes. Going beyond what a strictly precise depiction of the principal subject demands, Atget leaves a tiny space to either side of the centered image. Greenhorn photographers are always being instructed: "Get in closer, move up closer! What were you interested in? Is it exactly that? No? It is! Well then, center it bang in the middle and the rest can go hang." But the advice one has to give to a more experienced hand, one who knows how to "frame" his pictures, is far more subtle and arcane: "Let it breathe, don't cramp the image. Here, you need just a touch more space to give a sense of the world outside and to let the poetry of the place flow out and add something to the power of its volumes."

Atget is a master of this collusion between rigor and openness. Formal balance keeps to itself perfectly, yet, inside and towards the edges, there opens up another space which connects to the reality lying outside the photographic field. We are not here in the presence of a picture-maker whose subjects are but pretexts, but before a visual witness, a man who walks and who feels responsible for the image of an entire city through its myriad particularities.

Within the constraints of a career in which avant-garde provocation was utterly alien, Atget's kinship (in terms of plastic and poetical sense) with the great modernist movements such as Cubism and Surrealism is all the more astonishing. He did not reorganize our attitude to space, as did Stieglitz in his *Steerage*, but he portrayed instead the inner courtyards and narrow streets of the city as pure combinations of geometric volumes. Absorbing himself in the sturdy cornices, in the reliefs draped in shadow, in the gaps punched out for the windows, Atget transforms the vernacular architecture of Old Paris into an array of contrasting facets, putting us in mind of early Cubist paintings and photographs which are sustained by the precise imbrication of the planes.

Elsewhere — as a counterweight to such austere spatial constructions — a dream of melancholy walks abroad. Is Atget's Paris haunted? Without a hint of lyrical romanticism or pictorialist nobility, the great etcher Charles Meryon (1821–68) had also turned a penetrating eye to the solid volumes of the houses of Paris and the intensity of the shadows outlining their fortifications. The dark strokes of his burin went straight to the essential. Yet the intensity of his gaze was to get the better of his reason and, towards the end, he returned to his etching plates to conjure up figures of the dead who had until then remained unseen wandering in his mind but who now, naked and blanched, perched on the walls or floated high in the air.

Such visionary fantasies are foreign to Atget — at least for the most part, since there does exist one series that evokes phantoms in which the misted image of a figure appears through the glazed doors of a store. At a time when people were more convivial, the storekeepers, whenever they caught sight of Atget setting up his camera outside their shop, would come out and, after striking an advantageous pose for the photograph, start up a conversation. To do the series in question, whose repetitive nature could hardly be the fruit of chance alone, Atget had only to ask them to step back into the store and stand up very close to the shop-window so that their silhouette would not be swallowed entirely in the shadows. This highly deliberate approach lies at the opposite end of the spectrum from the equally purposeful series on local trades in which each figure is placed in bright sunlight in a patently professional pose. It was said of Victor Hugo that for him the mere act of seeing was somehow frightening. It might be said of Atget that with him the mere act of designating was somehow creative. The very act of showing — without even a trace of ostentation — already involves something wondrous. No rhetoric mediates the eloquence of a vista or the lyricism of the sky, just a calm intimacy with the presence of things. If certain powerful effects necessitated an evident act of single-mindedness — like placing a large camera on the ground, for instance — this was not done in order to introduce us to a world marshaled by imperious stylization, as is the case with so many great photographers (Bill Brandt comes to mind), but to encourage us to partake of the emotion that seeps from one particular place. Light itself — the very substance of photographic creation — keeps to its unassuming neutrality, stripped down to its intrinsic function, that of showing. In the sky, no clouds, no drama; now and again contrast is heightened on the stones, but only because that is how things are when the untamed sun beats down and settles within the hairline cracks of the old city.

Atget did not achieve the marvelous quality of his images by sleepwalking through life. Since Berenice Abbott, other photographers have demonstrated the truth of what she sensed were Atget's purposeful and conscious technical decisions. Yet the vastness of Atget's documentary project meant that he could reject formal excesses out of hand, to the point that today one might even talk of a Conceptual art. Strictly speaking, however, the expression "Conceptual art" is devoid of meaning. Since the eighteenth century, it has been accepted that, since art is essentially freedom, concepts have nothing to do with the artistic domain. Confusion persists thanks to the evident importance of what Kant termed the artistic idea. This is the intention of the work, the thought directed towards the realization of new material forms. The concept is all the more concept in that the idea turns back on itself. This is a necessity and an ideal for all things of a scientific nature. In art, however, the idea is only transitional, only a route to and from the work. Claude Lévi-Strauss has explained that art is always possessed of three aspects: project, elaboration, and communication, and further that these three aspects are always present in unequal proportions, depending on the periods, countries, and peoples concerned. Atget, far from contenting himself with a theoretical notion of photography, broadened the scope of his venture, to the point that, today, it has all the characteristics of a work of art. Yet he knew that the quality of the project itself presupposes that of each of the images.

He did not forget, of course, that his images were destined for others. The albums he compiled demonstrate that, quite apart from his own archives, he would have liked to publish on a number of subjects. His oeuvre was on the threshold of moving on to a further dimension: the book. This is the germ for what was to become a familiar procedure for modern creative photographers such as Walker Evans, Ralph Gibson, etc. By returning to his unrelenting project, Atget might have been able to go as far as to transform it, through page-by-page comparisons, into an Imaginary Museum incorporated within his immense oeuvre. It remains a dream we can entertain, although we know that destiny struck down the then obscure old man too soon.

Atget's central lesson was best grasped, illustrated, and transmitted by Walker Evans. Perhaps as early as 1929 in Paris, but certainly in 1930 once back in New York, Evans found confirmation of a dazzling intuition: "Art is useless, so it can never be a document. But it can readily take on the style of a document." There can exist a style that rejects "style" but which is thus all the more creative. There is a point at which the mere acceptance of the visible, in its most limpid, obviously present form, coincides with a new way of looking at the real. Here, observation and invention fuse at the very root. It is a point that lies deep down near the origin, and, of all the arts, only photography can sometimes reach it — as indeed Eugène Atget proved that it could.

Conscientious, methodical, objective, Atget lay aside not only the expressiveness the Romantics were so fond of but also the desire for originality that the moderns craved. His timeless gravity allows no aesthetic ideology to come between eye and external reality. This withdrawal from all definable artistic ambition strips bare both the poetics of space and formal equilibrium. The retreat of the aesthetic itself discloses a less artificial

notion of aesthetics. With an exhibition that does not concern itself with lineage or influence but instead with connections between works, that does not preoccupy itself with art history but instead with the Imaginary Museum (and which, therefore, can pass over a disciple as well-known as Berenice Abbott), it was right to begin with a notion that came late on the scene, yet which remains fundamental and all-embracing: the ready-made.

Atget was one who looked unflinchingly at what he saw, who placed himself in front of things. The epitome of the classical photographer, one who wants to convey neither a moment, nor an impression, but a thing; he separated mentally what had chosen to show from the rest. From this derived the unmediated exaltation of the solitary gas jet, which seems only the more present as pure visibility — that is to say, as a work of art. An un-intentional artwork (but it is difficult to be sure to what extent this is the case), it stands there, as a witness to an aesthetic of indifference which is therefore no more an aesthetic but which lays bare the very nerve center — as tender as a sharp pain — of what beauty is. These two notions, customarily inextricable, are here made distinct for us. When Renger-Patzsch in his turn photographs a gas jet, he does so in manner perhaps more lucidly intellectual (but again, can we be so sure?), yet, obeying Atget's tenets, he both presents and isolates.

The wrought-iron craftsman who made the famous bottle-rack knew what he was making, whether or not he might have called it art (and how can we know?) and any conversation he might have had with Duchamp would have been most edifying. Be that as it may, it is patently, glaringly obvious that the bottle-rack was chosen for what are astounding plastic qualities. There was no point in denying this fact. If pushed into a corner, Duchamp would confess: "It's not me that does the choosing ... It is I that am chosen." And what sincere artist of any period would not say the same of any one of his own pieces?

Thus, when Atget records the structure and clear-cut outlines of the sweep of a staircase, he is aware of entering into a one-to-one dialogue with an artisan-artist from the past concerning the forms themselves, quite independently of social considerations and hierarchies.

The Bechers are comparable to Atget in tackling the notion of the series. As with him, their whole enterprise is built up into an opus, and the individuality of each image is enhanced when extracted from their uniform alignment. Atget was a man of high culture, a lover of classical tragedy and romantic drama alike. If he had taken photographs in keeping with the Bechers' taste, they would have been of the Louvre's majestic colonnades or else of Nôtre-Dame cathedral bristling with gargoyles. As a photographer, however, he stood outside history, the unwitting prophet (but again, can we be so sure?) of a new era in which art arises — quite apart from its different periods or places of origin — from the confrontation of extremes.

When Atget photographed a grotesque mascaron on the fountain in the Rue de Grenelle, he did so in the same impassioned way that Walker Evans was to capture on film a tribal mask from the Metropolitan Museum. Thus four artists met — with the African being perhaps the most clear-sighted of all of them, though that too is unknowable.

When Atget photographed a series of tree trunks and roots (recently reclassified in the collections of the Bibliothèque Nationale) he applied — this time to the venerable theme of natural beauty — the spirit of bare statement that allows the object to emerge in total completeness (as with the ready-made). Since the eighteenth century, in addition to the traditional eulogies of nature's amiable charms, there has arisen a taste for its sublime grandeur. Atget now brought to it the power of a silence compact and dense, as unyielding as a tree trunk.

Atget lived at the time of the Cubist adventure, but he paid it no attention. That style, whose best examples are confined to the space of very few years, is only truly effective in painting, since at the outset, and before moving on to address the plasticity of planes and volumes, it concerned the problem of the painter's touch. Yet, if we place side-by-side reproductions of works by Picasso and Braque, or Lipchitz and Zadkine, and Paul Strand's close-ups of engines or many of the Paris courtyards taken by Atget, we feel ourselves in the presence of one and the same family of forms, of a kindred universe of coherence. Girded by contrasting facets of a raw, unadorned architecture, brutal in its volumes, all clear-cut planes, and pierced with yawning openings for windows, these cramped spaces resemble the descent into the innards of a machine. The beginning of the twentieth century witnessed a short-lived reconciliation between art and the machine — yet this was only the effect of a new receptivity to the implacable plenitude of forms in space that extended far beyond subject-matter.

The sturdy beams Dieter Appelt photographed for his loft sequence correspond to the four-square rhythms of the seventeenth-century staircases that Atget had explored. The mock-casual manner in which, with scant regard for the rules of classical unity, a photograph by Jacques Darche or Lee Friedlander slices the image in two with a vertical bar so as to enhance the tension between areas of space, perhaps finds in Atget its conscious or unconscious precedent (which is to us perhaps immaterial).

While the Cubists and a number of abstract artists were geometricizing the world, many-headed Surrealism was restructuring it as a dreamscape. In the area of Surrealist painting, however, we have become used to fearing the worst. The time has come, then, to proclaim in no uncertain terms that it is in photography — in the hands of masters such as Vilem Kriz, Clarence John Laughlin, and Jindřich Štyrský — that the supreme illustrations of the otherworldly are to be found. It is important, though perhaps not essential, that they were all admirers of Atget; but they were certainly all artists who experienced photography's potential to transmogrify reality through an ability to lend greater intensity to the mysterious presence of beings and to surprise us

through unexpected lighting effects, transparency, and juxtaposition that an indolent gaze would have missed. The enigmatic solitude of a statue in a park or of a horse waiting at the side of the kerb, is not first and foremost that of a three-dimensional object transformed into a sculpture in the manner of a gas jet, but an eerie presence that disquiets the world.

That the historical fact of conscious influence is of slender importance in the perspective of the Imaginary Museum should not lead us to belittle the interest of direct and premeditated exchanges between photographers when these take place in the artistic sphere. Walker Evans' frontality and the rejection of all effects auxiliary to the pure photographic data are positions derived from Atget's unfussy approach, while on occasion the American's urban perspectives are inspired by the near theatrical arrangements of some of the earlier photographer's compositions on old Paris squares that await the entrance of some character as yet unnamed. Atget surely had his former trade in mind when photographing the deserted squares of old Paris.

For the historian or psychologist this encounter between Eugène Atget and Walker Evans is one of naivete and lucidity joining forces in a single affirmation of purity. For an aesthetic approach directed towards the forms, however, the essential resides in the selfsame mastery of visual data devoid of pre-existent expressiveness. The fact that absence of style, the degree zero of the document, can be a style of its own, and even *the* photographic style par excellence, that a quiet presence, nothing more than the thing itself, can become the seat of an aesthetic emotion: this is what Evans makes plain and what Atget kept to himself, though he too could have done exactly the same thing.

A major paradox amounting to almost an unthinkable truth runs through the history of photography: that it is not because it offers a wealth of personal interpretations that photography has become an art form, but through its capacity to push our noses up against the contingent, against the "so it is" and the irremediably absurd. In painting, in sculpture too, dialogues of the highest stature have in the past taken place between artists — El Greco and Tintoretto, Manet and Velázquez, Rodin and Donatello. On a more modest though no less evident level, the photographic dialogue between Eugène Atget and Lee Friedlander resulted in a vision where the inevitable flattening out of the forms of real space was converted into a way of exalting the movement, tensions, and correspondences between them.

Atget, who knew how to focus on the many plastic qualities of the ramshackle areas of Paris, also knew how to convey in a masterly manner the broad, emphatic, eurythmical, and uncluttered spaces of the French garden. Equally sensitive to sites of this kind, Bruno Réquillart has taken fresh photographs of Atget's views, adding the subtle detachment of an artist supremely conscious of his modernity.

Some of Atget's finest works, depicting the park at Saint-Cloud in the 1920s for example, forestall all attempts at comparison. They enter the Imaginary Museum by a high and arduous path to commune together with the very greatest in art, independently of distinctions in time and place.

Art is in the same position as God in negative theology: none can state what God is, we can only say what he is not. Beauty in photography does not stem from the intrinsic interest of the subject, nor from fine sentiments, nor from pretty lines, nor from moving memories. Atget's work lies on an ineffable plane — perhaps owing to its dearth of "artistic" ambition (but how can we be sure?), but certainly thanks to its exemplary distance from styles and fashions. Although this occurred in the middle of a period driven by the notion of the avant-garde, Atget had already positioned himself — or at least found himself — outside and far beyond it. The visual problems that he both discovered and resolved were not subordinated to a preconceived aesthetic project: his aesthetic was not of distance but was coterminous with his everyday work. The problems he had were real ones, and he solved them. From that point on, his oeuvre visibly contains the germ of the directions that others were to exploit in a desire to appear original. Atget was known as an "eccentric" among his neighbors, but they should really have said "original."

To today's eyes, this position seems to have burning relevance, when the disappearance of any reference to aesthetic ideologies has at last given us the hope of acceding to an art that can be accepted for what it is.

JEAN-CLAUDE LEMAGNY

From "Naive Artist" to "Pioneer"
The Adventures of a Work of Artisan Origin

In 1975, shortly before his death in New Haven, the American photographer Walker Evans declared: "I do not like to look at too much of Atget's work because I am too close to that in style myself… It's a little residue of insecurity and fear of such magnificent style and strength."[1] This revealing confession represents the very last occasion on which one of the greatest American photographers of the twentieth century was to speak of the fascination exerted on him by the work of his French forerunner, who had passed away in Paris almost 50 years before. At the time of his death on August 4, 1927, not a word on Atget's death appeared in the press. In his lifetime, however, Atget had sold thousands of pictures, all sorts of "documents" as he called them, as much to Parisian institutions as to his many private buyers, such as artists and architects, among others.

Ironically Man Ray and the Paris Surrealists had discovered Atget's images just before he died and just a short while after his demise his works — whatever he might have wished for them — were propelled to the forefront of the international art scene.

The story of Atget's work, which started out as a trade, remains today untypical and extraordinary. To retrace its strange history is to recall a series of chance events and lucky breaks that contributed to his works being disseminated geographically, culturally, and aesthetically. From early on, his works had a decisive effect on the world of creative photography and formed the basis for its eventual renaissance. To re-use a term employed on the occasion of the International Atget Colloquium (organized at the Collège de France in 1985 by the French Association for the Promotion of Photographic Heritage[2]), Atget's "sons" are legion. Or, to be more precise, there are many who saw, and many who still see him, as a prime source of their inspiration.

Atget's Discovery by the Surrealists

Whenever the conversation turned to Atget, Man Ray would claim: "I discovered him!"[3] It was in the mid-1920s that the American artist first went to visit Atget (he lived just a few yards from his studio), purchasing around 50 photographs from him. In 1926, Man Ray organized the publication of works by Atget in the journal *La Révolution surréaliste*, the independent organ of the "Central Bureau of Surrealist Research." These appeared alongside texts by Louis Aragon, Robert Desnos, Antonin Artaud, Philippe Soupault, Michael Leiris, René Crevel, etc., as well as reproductions of works by Arp, Tanguy, De Chirico, and Picasso. Unlike the images by these artists, however, Atget's photographs were not credited. It was, however, the elderly photographer himself who insisted on his anonymity, telling Man Ray: "These are simply documents,"[4] and it was precisely as "documents" that these images were to make such an impression on Man Ray and the Surrealists.

As a fragment of reality devoid of cultural intention, the photographic document is a form which offers rich pickings for subjective interpretation. As with the "found object," it is perceived as a catalyst, as a source for that "delirium of interpretative association" envisaged by Salvador Dalí: "The reel with no thread [a detail in the corner of one of Atget's images reproduced unacknowledged in the Surrealist journal *Minotaure*] clamorously demands to be interpreted."[5] And indeed it was to be Surrealist interpretation and its out-of-context readings, in which the original was quite divorced from its function, that were to invest these photographic documents with meaning. Hence the cover of the seventh number of *La Révolution surréaliste* (June 15, 1926) was illustrated with a photo by Atget where the original title "The Eclipse" had been jettisoned to be replaced by the more ambiguous "Last Conversions."

Man Ray and the Surrealists did not approach Atget's pictures as artworks in their own right or on the same level as their own. They considered him rather as the "Douanier Rousseau of photography."[6] an unconscious *naive*, and it was in this guise that he was considered worthy of the honors of the movement. All the same, Man Ray's purchases of Atget photographs were far from indiscriminate. Quite apart from those showing houses of ill-repute and nudes, there appears a high

[1] John Szarkowski and Maris Morris Hambourg, *The Work of Atget*, vol. 4, *Modern Times*, New York: MoMA, 1985, p. 18.   [2] See, "Atget, père et fils," (Proceedings of the Atget Colloquium under the auspices of the Association française pour la diffusion du patrimoine photographique: Collège de France, June 14–15, 1985) in *Photographies*, extra number, March 1986, pp. 39–91.   [3] Paul Hill and Tom Cooper, "Interview: Man Ray," in *Camera*, 2, February 1975, p. 39; quoted from Paul Hill and Tom Cooper, *Dialogue with Photography*, London: Thames and Hudson, p. 17.   [4] Paul Hill and Tom Cooper, loc. cit., p. 40; quoted from Paul Hill and Tom Cooper, *Dialogue with Photography*, London: Thames and Hudson, p. 18.   [5] Salvador Dalí, "Psychologie non-euclideinne d'une photographie," in *Minotaure*, 7, 1935, p. 56.   [6] Robert Desnos' comparison (see "Eugène Atget" in *Le Soir*, September 1928) has been recycled many times, in particular by Albert Valentin, "Eugène Atget (1856–1927)" in *Variétés*, 8, December 15, 1928 and Waldemar George, "Photographies vision du monde," in *Arts et métiers graphiques*, 16, special photography number, 1930, p. 134.

proportion of store windows and of shop-fronts with dummies. These store windows, with their multiple reflections or superimposed images, remind us of the superpositions of which Surrealist photographers were so fond, as do a group of mannequins, despairingly stiff, and sometimes mutilated or else obscured by a reflection or by sharp cropping. In store windows, as on the sidewalk, the mannequins represent human simulacra, mimicking the gestures and attitudes of an absent human presence. Also, not far from Atget's photographs of corsets published in the *La Révolution surréaliste* in 1926, we meet other examples by De Chirico and, in an earlier number, by Vigneau.[7] In 1929, the first number of the avant-garde journal *Bifur* published a reproduction of a store front with a window-dresser's dummy photographed by Kertész whose work had been exhibited in conjunction with prints by Atget the previous year at the Salon des Indepéndants de la Photographie. An interest in mannequins also emerges in the work of the Czech painter Jindřich Štyrský, who resided in Paris from 1925 to 1928, knew Man Ray, and followed the Surrealist movement. Turning his hand to photography in 1934–35, Štyrský produced some photos of store windows and circuses that evoke a number of the Frenchman's images appearing in photographs that had been acquired by Man Ray. Mannequins occur too in the work of François Kollar who photographed unclothed examples in a couture house as illustrations to *La France travaille*. Dress dummies also proved of interest to Sasha Stone whose photograph entitled *Anatomie féminine avec mannequins désassemblés* appeared in the second number of *Bifur*. The German Hans Bellmer's photographs of disjointed dolls, published in 1934 in the journal *Minotaure*, are also informed by the idea of the mannequin. If, in his *Small History of Photography* of 1931, Walter Benjamin was retrospectively of the opinion that "Atget's Paris photos are the forerunners of Surrealist photography," this is because, beyond the thematic influences, Atget's images of a deserted "cleared-out city" dignified "a salutary estrangement between man and his surroundings,"[8] so important to the Surrealists.

ATGET AND THE EUROPEAN AVANT-GARDES

"Was he French or American?"[9] enquired Gustaf Stotz, the organizer of the 1929 "Film und Foto" exhibition held in Stuttgart. Four years after the anonymous publication of Atget's photographs in *La Révolution surréaliste*, his prints were hanging on picture rails alongside works from the international avant-garde arena and were included in the American section of the famous FIFO. What had happened in less than four years for Atget's unassuming documents to be co-opted into one of the most significant artistic events of the between-the-wars period and yet for his nationality to be uncertain to the curator?

If Man Ray claimed the "discovery" of Atget for himself, it was the American Berenice Abbott who became primarily responsible for publicizing his work, and it was she who had sent 11 photos by Atget, from those in her possession, with her own entry to the FIFO in 1929. Abbott had settled in Paris, as a young woman, in 1923. She had initially moved to the capital to study sculpture, but soon became Man Ray's assistant, responsible for printing. He initiated her into studio portraiture and the pupil was soon sufficiently popular to be able to open her own studio through which passed many a celebrity. It was certainly with Man Ray acting as the middleman that in 1925 Abbott first saw photographs by Atget.[10] She bought a few prints from Atget and encouraged him to sit for her, producing two now famous portraits of the photographer, one in full-face and the other in profile. When she wanted to show them to him, however, it was too late: she found that the old man had just died.

Less than a year later she brought up his entire studio stock. At the time it appeared to interest nobody in France — neither the institutions for which Atget had regularly provided documents, nor (with the possible exception of Florent Fels[11]) his private clients. It was thus to the American Abbott that Atget's friend and legatee André Calmettes entrusted a collection that included negatives that he had not transferred to the Archives Photographiques, as well as the prints in albums that the photographer had kept for reference. He also handed over an address book ("répertoire") in which Atget had noted his clients' contact details and the bound album *L'Art dans le vieux Paris*. In all, this amounted to around 1,500 glass-plate negatives, as well as nearly 10,000 prints. With Calmettes' aid, Abbott also put together the basic elements of a biography[12] of Atget. Very soon it occurred to her to write a monograph on the photographer, the book being published simultaneously in French, English, and German in 1930.[13] Abbott later recorded the profound effect Atget's work had on her: "Their impact was immediate and tremendous. There was a sudden flash of recognition, the shock of realism unadorned," recalling the day she first saw them. "The subjects were not sensational, but nevertheless shocking in their very familiarity. The real world, seen with wonderment and surprise, was mirrored in each print. Whatever means Atget used to project the image did not intrude between subject and observer."[14]

Atget's photographs were utterly at odds with the Pictorialist aesthetic raised at that time to the status of an official art photography both in the Salons and by the press. For the Pictorialists — the most famous representatives in France being Robert Demachy and Constant Puyo — a strictly referential photograph could be no more than a mechanical record and absolutely never a work of art. In producing their photographs,

[7] On this subject, see Thomas Michael Gunther, "Man Ray and Co.: la fabrication d'un buste," *Colloque Atget*, op. cit., pp. 66–73. Forty-six of Atget's prints which had previously belonged to Man Ray are also reproduced; see also, Alain Buisine, "Vitrines et simulacres" and "Viduité" in *Eugène Atget ou la mélancolie en photographie*, Nîmes: Jacqueline Chambon, 1994, pp. 67–82, and pp. 183–92.   [8] Walter Benjamin, "A Small History of Photography," in *One-Way Street and other Writings*, London: Verso, 1979 (repr. 2000), p. 251.   [9] Quoted by Olivier Lugon in *Le "style documentaire" dans la photographie allemande et américaine des années vingt et trente*, doctorate thesis under the supervision of Pierre Vaisé, University of Geneva, 1994. See a letter by Gustaf Stotz, the organizer of the exhibition, to Berenice Abbott, owner of the photographs by Atget, April 8, 1929, "Was he French or American?"   [10] See Hank O'Neal, *Berenice Abbott: American Photographer*, New York: McGraw Hill, 1982.
[11] See Françoise Reynaud, "Préface," in *Berenice Abbott, Changing New York, Une ville en mouvement, 1935-1939*, Paris: Hazan/Paris Musées, 1999, p. 13.   [12] André Calmettes sent at least four letters to Abbott between 1928 and 1929. The letters are presently housed in the Atget Archives at the Museum of Modern Art, New York.
[13] French edition: *Atget, photographe de Paris* (with a preface by Pierre Mac Orlan), Paris: Joncquières, 1930; American edition, New York: Weyhe, 1930; German edition, *Eugène Atget, Lichtbilder* (preface by Camille Recht), Paris/Leipzig, 1930; 96 photographs.   [14] Berenice Abbott, *The World of Atget*, New York: Horizon Press, 1964, p. viii.

they preferred artistic processes, in particular gum bichromate printing which allowed for retouching and made it possible to achieve a pictorial quality close to that of engraving or drawing. Their subjects were also intended to evoke academic painting and ranged from nudes and landscapes to portraiture.[15]

It was in opposition to the dominance of Pictorialist aesthetics that the First Salon des Indépéndants de la Photographie was set up. It presented works by Berenice Abbott, Man Ray, Germaine Krull, André Kertész, Paul Outerbridge, and other photographers from what were then thought of as the "anti-conformist and revolutionary"[16] figures of the time. It was in the company of such cosmopolitan photographers that — on the initiative of Berenice Abbott and perhaps Man Ray, and less than one year after his death — Atget's work was exhibited for the first time.

The images by the as yet unknown photographer attracted all the more curiosity on the part of the critics since they were associated with prints by Nadar. The enthusiastic welcome they received exceeded even that normally reserved for that celebrated photographer. In October of the same year Atget's work was shown yet again, once more at Berenice Abbott's initiative, though this time in an exhibition at the Brussels gallery L'Époque.[17] Even his name, which until then had often been misspelt by the critics (Adget, Atger, and Atgat), was beginning to become better known. The following year, the presence of eleven works in the international "Film und Foto"[18] show at Stuttgart (May 18 to July 7, 1929) assimilated his work with that of other avant-garde photographers. Sent in by Abbott as an annex to her own entry, Atget's prints thus appeared in the American section of the exhibition in a room curated by Weston and Steichen, a fact which explains the confusion over his nationality. A trilingual book with the air of a manifesto, Foto-Auge,[19] that was published in parallel with the FIFO, opens with a photograph by Atget (Boulevard de Strasbourg, Corsets, 1912). Conjointly represented at the "Fotografie der Gegenwart" exhibition, Atget is henceforth referred to as a precursor of the New Objectivity (Neue Sachlichkeit) and is associated with the Americans as a counterexample to the New Vision whose extravagance was beginning to wear thin.

In his Small History of Photography of 1931, Walter Benjamin offers confirmation of the Frenchman's role as a forerunner when he notes that the avant-garde photographs in which there appear so many close-ups "are nothing but a literary refinement of themes that Atget discovered."[20] Benjamin's text on Atget is moreover illustrated with photographs by Germaine Krull, images in which the French critic Paul Fierens had already seen the stamp of the "Atget tradition" in 1929. Though Atget's images provided some backing for this

New Objectivity, they were just as quickly being seen to bring it into question and — as Olivier Lugon[21] has explained — "give the impression that the spectacular cropping used by proponents of New Objectivity was decorative and artificial." Thus, at the end of 1929, or at the very latest in 1930, New Objectivity was charged with mannerism and its academicism and formalism denounced.

In comparison with New Objectivity's overhasty and contradictory borrowings, Atget fulfilled the function of a veritable "cameraman of intelligibility"[22] who could serve to articulate the questions and challenges thrown up by modernity. Mediated by Berenice Abbott, Atget's assimilation into the avant-garde formed an integral part of a modernist current that was rediscovering the functional and practical uses of photography: scientific and utilitarian photography and even family snapshots combined to give rise to a novel and inventive approach to form that betrayed an interest in documents of all kinds as opposed to more artistic work.

The emergence of Atget's work furthermore occurred at a time of burgeoning interest in nineteenth-century exponents, just when the first steps were being taken in the written history of photography, probably linked to the recent exploration at the hands of the avant-garde itself of a variety of photographic processes. As modernism itself unfolded, so it started to compose a history for itself. The tendency, though observable in Europe, was characteristically widespread in the United States, where the return to the past — that went in hand in hand with the unearthing of so-called "ancestors" (a label that was posthumously applied to Atget) — sanctioned a new approach to the field opened up by the upcoming generation of American documentary photographers.

ATGET'S WORKS EMIGRATE TO AMERICA

Packed in upwards of 20 wooden cases, the Atget collection crossed the Atlantic in the spring of 1929, eventually coming to rest in Berenice Abbott's New York apartment. Leaving her flourishing portrait business in Paris far behind, Abbott began to take photographs of the city in a documentary approach following Atget's model. Her new activities in the field of photography, however, did not put a stop to her continuing promotion of Atget's work in her native land. All her good work was eventually rewarded, as shown by a 1938 article which states that, thanks to her efforts, "overnight Atget climbed into history."[23]

A few months after her return to the United States, Abbott wrote her debut article on Atget for the journal Creative Art, presenting him as a "modern forerunner"[24] whose work had already revolutionized photography. His images open a whole "new world in the realm of creative expression." Introduced to the work of the

[15]In the United States, this trend is exemplified by Alfred Stieglitz and his journal, Camera Work.   [16] Georges Waldemar, "L'Art photographique" in La Presse, October 16, 1928.   [17] P. L. "L'Exposition de la photographie à la Galerie L'Époque," in Variétés, Brussels, November 15, 1928.   [18] Film und Foto. International Ausstellung des deutschen Werkbunds, exhibition catalogue with texts by Gustav Stotz, Edward Weston, and others, Stuttgart, 1929; and reissued in facsimile, New York: Arno Press, 1979.   [19] foto-auge/oeil et photo/eye and photo, text by Franz Roh. Franz Roh and Jan Tschichold, eds. Stuttgart: Akademischer Verlag Fritz Wedekind, 1929   [20] Walter Benjamin, op. cit., p. 250.   [21] Olivier Lugon, op cit.   [22] Dominique Baqué, "À l'origine du modernisme, Atget," in Les documents de la modernité. Anthologie de textes sur la photographie de 1919 à 1939, Nîmes: Jacqueline Chambon, 1993, p. 398.   [23] Robert W. Marks, "Chronicler of Our Times," in Coronet, December 1938, p. 166.   [24] Berenice Abbott, "Eugène Atget," in Creative Art, vol. 5, no. 3, September 1929, p. 651; quoted in John Szarkowski, The World of Atget, vol. 4, p.15.   [25] Walker Evans, "The Reappearance of Photography," in Hound and Horn, October–December 1931, pp. 126.   [26] Ansel Adams, "Photography: an Early Master," in The Fortnightly, vol. 1, no. 5, November 6, 1931, p. 25; quoted by John Szarkowski, "Understandings of Atget," in The Work of Atget vol. 4, Modern Times, New York: MoMA, 1985, p.18.   [27] It should be noted that the number of photographs in America fostered this twofold reputation of the photographer: the Abbott collection was acquired in 1968 by

Frenchman by Abbott herself, Walker Evans portrayed Atget in "The Reappearance of Photography" in much the same way as an isolated precursor in a what was "a period of utter decadence in photography."[25] Then, at the end of 1931, Ansel Adams also wrote an article on him, describing him as "representing perhaps the earliest expression of true photographic art."[26] Just as Atget's work had bolstered Neue Sachlichkeit in Germany, so it was to underwrite the efforts of a new generation of American photographers for whom he was to become *the* father of the documentary. Atget is thus dually considered as not only an "ancestor" but also a forerunner,[27] and his photographs were exhibited in conjunction with those of other "ancestors"[28] such as Brady (who had also been rediscovered by Abbott), Nadar, and Hill, or else compared to photographs of the American documentary school.[29]

In September 1930, Atget's prints were part of an exhibition of photography mounted by Lincoln Kirstein at Harvard. The show heralded an important turning-point in the history of documentary photography in the United States. Breaking wholly with the Stieglitz tradition, it provided a forum not just for art photography (though it did feature Stieglitz himself, as well as Steichen and Strand), but followed its German predecessor in incorporating scientific, commercial, and press photography. Moreover introductory material in the catalogue actually referred to *Foto-Auge*. While it certainly mirrored the diversity of the FIFO, the exhibition offered a fresh perspective and some new models. The catalogue passed over avant-garde experimentation (only a few photomontages and photograms were presented), stressing instead the documentary quality of photography. Countering Stieglitz's aesthetic[30] and using Atget as a exemplum, the exhibition advocated the pure "clarity of the documentary form" and valorized a new American generation whose work was close to Atget's.

Held a year after the Harvard exhibition, the show at the Albright Art Gallery endorsed Kirstein's position, as well as enlisting two other founding fathers: Nadar and Hill. While Lincoln Kirstein was supporting American photographers through his journal *Hound and Horn*, from 1931 they were also defended by the gallery of Julien Levy,[31] who the previous year had furthered the first exhibition of Atget prints in the United States. In the last of the four volumes[32] he has devoted to Atget, John Szarkowski provides an "official" rollcall of the photographer's "documentary" descendents that lists the names of Berenice Abbott, Walker Evans, Brassaï, André Kertész, Henri Cartier-Bresson, and Manuel Alvarez-Bravo. Szarkowski also shows that the new tradition of

photography set in motion by Atget survives in more recent photographs by Garry Winogrand, Robert Frank, Lee Friedlander, and others. Nevertheless Atget owes his enduring posterity above all to the two very different trail-blazers of the new American documentary photography: Berenice Abbott and Walker Evans.

Abbott, not content simply to publicize the French photographer's work, also made his approach her own. Applying it to New York City, she declared in 1931: "What Eugene Atget did for Paris I want to do for New York,"[33] while the press described her as New York's answer to Atget. Walker Evans[34] for his part overcame the ambivalence between art and document that had permeated Atget's whole oeuvre by forging what he termed the "documentary style."[35] Evans and Abbott met in 1929, the year in which both started to take photographs of New York. It is also probably around this time that Abbott first showed Evans photographs by Atget.[36] He was already compared to Atget on the occasion of his first New York exhibition in 1931.[37] Their earliest New York work still shows the hallmarks of the European "New Vision" style. Using small-format cameras, they favored oblique and inverted compositions that continued to extol symbols of modernity, such as skyscrapers, suspension bridges, and metal structures. Nonetheless, Atget's influence is discernable even in these early works. In a few of Evans' photographs, for example, there appear storefronts, deserted streets, and interiors. The albums Abbott was later to present as "notebooks" also include store-windows and various artisan trades, and display an attention to the minutiae of urban space that owes much to the Frenchman's lead. At this stage, the formative influence was primarily a thematic one. In the eyes of the new American generation, among the subjects to which Atget's example gave the most support was architectural documentation, a phenomenon which around 1931 was to trigger a new departure in the work of both Abbott and Evans and convince them to start using a large-format view camera in their photographs of New York and Victorian houses. Cumbersome and unwieldy, this type of camera did not facilitate acrobatic views but did ensure greater clarity of detail.

Both photographers share numerous features with Atget on technical, formal, and aesthetic levels. That, however would seem to be the intention lying behind their photographic project that shows his influence at its strongest. Atget's work was motivated by his desire to record a gradually vanishing Paris. Evans' motivation was the old Victorian houses tumbling down more or less between two clicks of the shutter[38] that motivated this shift to a new style. Explaining it later, Evans referred to

MoMA, while the Atget photographs belonging to Man Ray passed to the photographer Beaumont Newhall for George Eastman House.   [28] In March 1930, the Ancestors show in the Ayer Galleries in Philadelphia included both Brady and Atget, presenting them as joint founders of modern photography. The following year, the Julien Levy gallery held an exhibition called Nadar and Atget, Old French Photographers.   [29] In 1930, Atget's photographs were juxtaposed with Abbott's own work (at the exhibition in the New York Weyhe Gallery in which Julien Levy was working), an association which was revived at a later date. The exhibitions at Harvard (1930), and the Albright Art Gallery (1931) pursued the comparison with the new generation of American documentary photographers. In 1939, an exhibition called Eugène Atget was presented by the Photo-League of New York. The following year, his photographs were shown once more at the Julien Levy gallery, but this time exhibited with shots of New Orleans by Clarence John Laughlin.   [30] For Walker Evans, "Stieglitz's veritably screaming aestheticism, his personal artiness, veered many younger camera artists to the straight documentary style; to the documentary approach for itself alone, not for journalism"; "We got a school of anti-art photography out of these protestations." Walker Evans, "Photography" in *Quality. Its Image in the Arts* (ed. Louis Kronenberger), New York: Atheneum, 1969, pp. 170 and 206.   [31] Evans and Abbott showed there a number of times: Evans in February 1932, with George Platt Lynes, and also in April 1935, with Henri-Cartier Bresson and Manuel Alvarez-Bravo, in the exhibition, Documentary and Anti-Graphic Photography, and Abbott in October 1932.   [32] John Szarkowski, "Understandings of Atget", op. cit., pp. 9–33.   [33] See "Photographing New York is the Big Ambition of Berenice Abbott," in *The New York Sun*, October 5, 1934 (Archives Berenice Abbott, Commerce Graphics, East Rutherford, New Jersey).   [34] Gilles Mora, *Walker Evans*, Paris: Belfond/Paris Audiovisuel, 1989, p. 53.   [35] Leslie Katz, "Interview with Walker Evans," in *The Camera Viewed*, New York: E. F. Dutton, 1979, p. 127. For supplementary information on the notion of the "documentary style" in Evans, see

Proust, explicitly stating that he was "interested in what you see that is passing out of history."[39] Abbott too was concerned with preserving "many of the fast disappearing records of early New York."[40] Her *Changing New York* project stemmed from a preoccupation with the preservation of history. Her goal was to record images of the ever-changing city "for the future." In a note dating from 1961, intended for a new edition of his *American Photographs*, Evans once more asserted that he had always been "interested in what any present time will look like as the past."[41] Evans and Abbott were not content, however, simply to record remnants from a bygone age as Atget had done before them. Their idea was to extend the project to an entire city and to incorporate its most modern aspects, on the understanding that everything is susceptible to change and eventually deterioration. They thought of themselves as "archeologists" for the future. Abbott, a partisan of "historical photography,"[42] also invoked "posterity" when elucidating her own photographic oeuvre. Such an attitude finds an echo in more contemporary photographic work, such as that of Bernd and Hilla Becher in Germany who for their part maintain that: "Our real problem is the struggle against time."[43]

ATGET AND PARIS

As John Szarkowski stressed during his contribution to the Atget Colloquium at the Collège de France, in America it was photographers who did most for Atget's work. In France, the process mainly involved conservators, who were to exhibit photographs by Atget selected from their collections. France lagged behind the United States in this respect, however, with no exhibition at all in the photographer's native land during the first few years of the partial exile of Atget's oeuvre across the Atlantic. The notion of compiling a history of photography, however, was gaining ground: in 1934, the critic Louis Cheronnet proposed creating a museum of photography which might ward off the threat of the dispersal of national heritage (Abbott having acquired the Atget collection, for example), and which would set aside a "whole room" devoted to "Atget, that simple soul, that Douanier Rousseau, that ingenuously genial hawker."[44]

Atget's prints, however, were not shown in France until 1941, on the occasion of an exhibition at the Musée Carnavalet, in Paris, entitled "Vues de Paris et petits métiers," devoted to photographs of the capital and of its more picturesque artisan crafts. They were displayed in conjunction with Paris photographs by Marville and Vert. Almost 25 years later, the Musée des Arts Décoratifs in Paris incorporated photographs by Atget in an exhibition covering a century of the art entitled, "Un Siècle de Photographie, de Nièpce à Man Ray."

In 1978 — six years after the Atget retrospective at New York's MoMA — it was the turn of the Archives Photographiques de la Direction de l'Architecture to display a number of the Atget photographs in its possession. Although these were in fact modern prints taken from the original negatives, the show was the first in France to be devoted solely to Atget (the exhibition was, moreover, a traveling one).

Since the 1980s, the Musée Carnavalet has been singularly successful in publicizing its Atget holdings, presenting a number of his albums as separate publications, including *Intérieurs parisiens artistiques, pittoresques et bourgeois* and *Petits métiers*. Gradually, collections in the Île-de-France *département* have also been bringing to light its own holdings (on Versailles and Sceaux).

As we have shown, Atget's prints are almost always associated with the theme of Paris and presented in accordance with an approach one might qualify as "topographic," not only in terms of the urban layout (the images are presented divided into *quartiers*[45]) but also with respect to the work itself (as in the various albums). Of all the French photographers to invoke Atget's name, Robert Doisneau is surely the most famous today. Recently christened collectively as "Humanists," all Atget's French "sons" share Paris as their chosen photographic subject and show working-class areas of the city from a poetic, intimate point of view. Atget's Parisian descendants first discovered his photographs through the monograph entitled *Atget photographe de Paris*,[46] brought out in France by the publisher Jonquières. As André Jammes has demonstrated, the photographs included in this book were selected both by Berenice Abbott (probably with Man Ray's help) and Jonquières, though the choice was also informed by commercial criteria.[47]

In this way, Atget's "modern-looking" prints (store fronts, mannequins, etc.), for the most part realized toward the end of his life, were shown cheek-by-jowl with more strictly documentary pieces in order to satisfy a widespread demand for pictures of old Paris. In this respect, *Atget photographe de Paris* was the source of a "host of photographic books on the City of Light in the 1930s"[48] foremost among which was *Paris de nuit*[49] published in 1933 and illustrated with 62 photographs by Brassaï. It was quite possibly the Hungarian photographer André Kertész, whose works had been exhibited together with Atget's in 1928, who had first prompted Brassaï to take photographs of Paris at night. Kertész, whose book *Paris*[50] appeared a year after Brassaï's, had like him fled the government of Admiral

Gilles Mora, op. cit.   [36] According to James Stern who knew Evans the latter probably first saw Atget photographs in November 1929; see James Stern, "Walker Evans 1903–1975: A Memoir," in *London Magazine*, vol. 17, no. 3, August–September 1977, p. 5.   [37] M. F. Agha, "Photography," a text on the invitation card to Margaret Bourke-White, Ralph Steiner, Walker Evans. Photographs by Three Americans, John Becker Gallery, New York, April 18 to May 8, 1931.   [38] As reported by Lincoln Kirstein, 1933.   [39] Leslie Katz, "Interview with Walker Evans," in *Art in America*, 1971, p. 87; quoted in *Photography in Print: Writings from 1816 to the Present* (ed. Vicki Goldberg), New York: Simon and Schuster, 1981, p. 365.   [40] Letter from Berenice Abbott to Hareinge Scholle, Director of the Museum of the City of New York, November 16, 1931.   [41] Quoted in John T. Hill, *Walker Evans at Work*, New York: Harper and Row, 1982, p. 151.   [42] See on this point, Olivier Lugon's thesis quoted above.   [43] Quoted by Gilles Mora in "Walker Evans, Lee Friedlander, Bernd et Hilla Becher de l'archive à la typologie," in *Vive les modernités* (Rencontres internationales de la photographie d'Arles), Arles: Actes Sud, 1999, p. 168.   [44] Quoted by Dominique Bacqué, op. cit., p. 496.   [45] These observations still apply today, in particular with respect to publications; see in particular the *Atget Paris* anthology first brought out by Hazan in 1992 with a preface by Laure Beaumont-Maillet.   [46] Ibid.   [47] See André Jammes, "La pate à modeler," in *Atget Colloquium*, op. cit., pp. 117–19.   [48] See Thomas Michael Gunther, "Man Ray and Co.: la fabrication d'un buste," *Atget Colloquium*, op. cit., p. 68.   [49] *Paris de nuit* (with photographs by Brassaï and a text by Paul Morand), Paris: Arts et Métiers graphiques, 1933.   [50] *Paris* (with photographs by Kertész and a text by Pierre Mac Orlan), Paris: Plon, 1934.   [51] Robert Doisneau, "Atget! je peux vous poser une question!" in *Atget Colloquium*, op. cit., p. 113. It should be recalled here that the figure of Atget aroused considerable interest in France, as much among critics and photographers as among historians. Jean Leroy's work on Atget's biography, begun in 1962 and continuously updated, is worthy of especial mention.   [52] Brassaï, "Mes souvenirs

Horthy to settle in the mid-1920s at Montparnasse, at the time Atget's own quarter. Brassaï saw Atget as his "spiritual father," devoting an article to his memory in 1969. Unlike Doisneau, who created for himself a "mythical Atget" (even calling on the assistance of a handwriting expert to elucidate his mysterious personality),[51] Brassaï had the opportunity of actually meeting the 69-year-old Atget. He tells how he first saw Atget's photographs at Zborovski the art dealer's in Montparnasse. The old man introduced himself and offered to show him some prints. "I was filled with wonder on seeing these photographs for the first time: the streets and alleyways of Paris, store fronts, dingy courtyards, and concierges' lodges; costermongers, brothels, streetwalkers, old shop-signs, barrowmen, and hawkers — images that bring back the very essence of Paris and from which its very smell would rise...."[52] This 1969 article was illustrated with photographs by Brassaï that he selected himself with an eye to their kinship with Atget's work. Robert Doisneau, in an article he penned on Atget in 1986, sets out to invite still more explicit comparisons, juxtaposing two of his photographs ("First Reportage at the Flea Market," 1931 and "Zoniers in Gentilly") with two pictures by Atget ("16 Rue du Petit-Thouars, Shop" and "Porte d'Italie, Zoniers, 13e" [arrondissement]). In fact, Doisneau could have chosen to couple dozens of other photographs of this type. He certainly shared Brassaï's avowed admiration for the "banal subjects disdained by art photographers but which were infused with meaning and which brought to our attention a hitherto unsung beauty."[53] For Doisneau, Atget was also the first to pace the "backstreets of the great city, and farther out still, into the outskirts, where he became the unique spectator of a drama played out by the laboring classes against a backdrop of which the elite could know nothing."[54] Finally, for Brassaï as much as for Doisneau, Atget's analytical approach fractures and fragments the city into myriad images, presenting a new view of Paris which breaks completely with the monumental and eulogizing vision fostered by those nineteenth-century photographers who, unlike Atget, were employed on state commissions intended to ennoble the city as it underwent its restructuring and modernization.[55] If Atget rubs shoulders with such figures in photographic family trees it is simply because they share a common subject: Paris. As far as the history of Parisian iconography is concerned Atget was the successor to nineteenth-century photographers, just as Doisneau, René-Jacques, Izis, Willy Ronis, and others were to follow in his wake. Nonetheless, on the strictly photographic level (since a photograph cannot be reduced to what it depicts), works by the "Humanists" are as far from Atget's as — in certain respects at least — his own are from photographs by nineteenth-century exponents. Atget's relatively neutral images are, for instance, totally immune to the sentimentality of the "Humanists."

This "French" approach to Atget's oeuvre also informs the way certain photographers have retraced the master's footsteps and actually reproduced images from his work. This exercise — one in which Robert Doisneau indulged in the past — is regularly given more up-to-date treatment by other photographers, Daniel Queynet being one of its most rigorous exponents.

CONCLUSION

Atget's life's work was vast and many-faceted. No overriding aesthetic ambition presided over its creation. On the contrary, its author remained in the background, preferring to remain anonymous to such an extent that his photographs might well have never left the realm of the archive. Where would Atget's work be today had André Calmettes simply sold or donated the holdings from the studio to one or other of the institutions of Paris? For Atget's photography to become better known, very different figures would have had to intervene, but they would have had to have been the right ones: for it was neither the Surrealists — the majority of whom were men of a literary bent — nor museum staff, nor the critics who did most to popularize his extraordinary oeuvre, but photographers. Moreover, these were cosmopolitan photographers, American for the most part, who had trained in the Paris of Roaring Twenties and who had first turned their hand to a variety of other artistic disciplines.[56] These figures were themselves out of step with the art photography tendencies of the time. For them to become conscious of Atget's work a series of coincidences had to occur: not only did chance have it that Man Ray and Atget were near-neighbors, but a figure like Berenice Abbott had also to become Man Ray's assistant. A number of other remarkable factors played a part in Atget's growing recognition: the partiality shown by the Surrealists for photographic documents; the avant-garde taste for functional photography, particularly in Germany; a fledgling interest in documentary techniques; and, finally, the creation of a history of photography that led to its "ancestors" being unearthed. The destiny of Atget's work provides evidence that "the aesthetic dimension of works made by an artisan is entirely independent of the aesthetic intentions of its creator."[57] In this sense the joint exhibition of Abbott and Atget held at the Musée Carnavalet in 1999 is indicative of the new ways of showing and seeing Atget's photographs in France. In the past, his images were presented primarily as documents to do with Paris, as if their attraction was confined solely to their portrayal of the capital. Perhaps this was due to an unspoken desire to disregard the American "diaspora" of Atget's work and to underscore the photographer's Gallic origins. His native land perhaps remained too close to the theme to look at them with an aesthetic eye, even though the history of Atget's work and its influences had been paving the way for precisely this approach for nearly 70 years.

LUCE LEBART

sur E. Atget, P. H. Emerson et Alfred Stieglitz," in Camera, year 48, no. 1, January 1969, pp. 4–13.   [53] Ibid.   [54] Robert Doisneau, op. cit., p. 114.   [55] See, Alain Buisine, "Le Paris des photographs" and "Habitabilités," in Eugène Aget ou la mélancolie de la photographie, Nîmes: Jacqueline Chambon, 1994, pp. 83–99 and pp. 143–47.   [56] Before becoming a photographer Abbott had spent time as a sculptor. Walker Evans was fascinated by Flaubertian realism and had contemplated a literary career, while Man Ray of course represents the epitome of this type of interdisciplinary approach.   [57] Alain Buisine, op. cit., p. 55.

*"Perhaps deep down,
I'm nothing but an old street singer"*
FRIEDRICH NIETZSCHE

Eugène Atget, *13, galerie Vivienne, Rampe* (Staircase), 1906 • Bernhard & Hilla Becher, *Tour de réfrigération* (Cooling Tower), 1967

Eugène Atget, *Arc-boutant de l'église Saint-Séverin* (Flying Buttress of the Church of Saint-Séverin), 1902

Bernhard & Hilla Becher, *Haut-fourneau* (Blast Furnace), 1969

Walker Evans, *Negro Church, South Carolina*, 1936

Eugène Atget, *2, rue des Haudriettes, "Au bon coin"*, 1908

31

Eugène Atget, *Rampe* (Staircase), *269, rue Saint-Jacques*, 1905

Eugène Atget, *Rampe* (Staircase), *21, rue du Cherche-Midi*, 1906

Eugène Atget, *Grue au pont du Louvre* (Crane at the Louvre Bridge), s.d.

Albert Renger-Patzsch, *Grue géante* (Giant Crane), *Hambourg*, 1929

Eugène Atget, *Jardin du Luxembourg, Bec de gaz* (Gas-Lamp), s.d.

Albert Renger-Patzsch, *Lampadaire* (Street Lamp), 1930

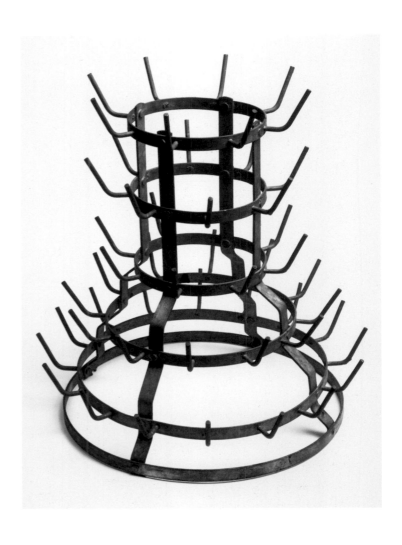

Marcel Duchamp, *Porte-bouteilles* (Bottle Rack), 1961

Eugène Atget, *Rampe* (Staircase), *5, rue de Montmorency*, 1908 • Eugène Atget, *Rampe* (Staircase), *57, rue de Varenne*, s.d.

Eugène Atget, *38, quai de Bourbon, enseigne de tabac* (Tobacconist's Shop Sign), 1901-1902

Walker Evans, *Tin Relic* (Chutes d'étain), 1930

Eugène Atget, *Détail de la fontaine de la rue de Grenelle par Bouchardon* (Detail of the Fountain in the rue de Grenelle by Bouchardon), 1907

Walker Evans, *African Mask* (Masque africain), 1935

43

Eugène Atget, *Parc de Saint-Cloud*, 1909-1911

Eugène Atget, *Parc de Saint-Cloud*, 1909-1911

45

Eugène Atget, *Parc de Saint-Cloud,* 1909-1911

The Trees in the Park at Saint-Cloud
in the Collections of the Bibliothèque Nationale de France
or
The Photographer and the Conservator

While Eugène Atget was still alive, libraries and museums — above all those of Paris — constituted one of his most important groups of clients. Either directly or else through the intermediary of print-dealers (such as Rapilly and later Le Garrec for the Bibliothèque Nationale), these institutions acquired considerable quantities of his photographs. From 1900 to 1927, the Department of Prints and Photography of the Bibliothèque Nationale de France enriched its collection of views of the architecture, the decorative arts, and the local trades of the capital with thousands of images. At that time no one would have dreamt of considering Atget as an artist. He himself was of much the same opinion, maintaining that the pictures he supplied — at prices varying from 1 to 3 francs — were no more than documents.

According to a now widely accepted account, the inherent beauty of Atget's images, which had until that time been unthinkingly purchased as something quite different from what they represent in our eyes, was first perceived and first understood in the milieu around Man Ray, Berenice Abbott, and the Surrealists. What might seem to us as a mistaken lack of appreciation did not affect Atget alone, however. Prior to him, all nineteenth-century photography had been treated in much the same way: the photographic documents acquired by the Bibliothèque Nationale from 1853 were paid for as if they were just that, documents, and were only later turned, through a fortuitous alchemical transformation in the history of taste, into works of art. In the case of the photographs acquired from Maxime Ducamp in 1853, or Raoult in 1878, it could hardly be expected that a contemporary, even with a far-sightedness verging on clairvoyance, could have possibly comprehended what we see today in such images.

As for the prints sold by Atget himself, his choice of subject — for the most part views of "old Paris" — simply offered confirmation of this utilitarian approach. It is only since Man Ray that we have become aware that such views can be read on two or even three levels. We now also know that Atget's work was concerned with subjects less easily decoded than the picturesque inventory of the capital, such as the albums on the *Zoniers* and the *Fortifications* that the Bibliothèque acquired in 1915. Although the manner of selecting these works remains obscure (the archives of the department are unfortu-

nately silent on the matter), we have to concede at least that the concept of documentation was very fluid and that our predecessors were able to follow Atget's work as it evolved towards more varied subjects and more inventive treatments of the image.

The laborious task of locating and classifying the historical photographs held by the department resulted in the recent rediscovery, in 1995, of a group of thirty-nine photographs by Atget. These studies of trees in the park at Saint-Cloud cannot have been considered as a source of information on the park itself: the "full-length portraits" of trees, or their details (roots or trunks), the studies of copses or thickets, tell us nothing about the overall topography of the place. If the words "St Cloud" in Atget's own handwriting did not systematically appear in pencil on the back of each print, it would have been absolutely impossible to pinpoint their location.[1]

These photographs, then called "studies after nature," were doubtless destined to supply artists, another group of Atget's clients. This category of photographs, large quantities of which had, since 1851, entered the department by means of copyright deposit, was not in principle acquired for any other reason. The question arises as to how such a group, which according to the criteria of the time had little or no value, could possibly have been obtained by the library.

Perhaps Jean Vallery-Radot in 1923 — at the time a very young conservator who had been recruited as recently as 1920 and entrusted with this kind of minor negotiation — had begun to feel some interest in, or even acquire a taste for, Atget's photographic work. Or do we have to resign ourselves to the fact that this exceptional group of photographs, which were never acquired by any other institution, formed part of a "job lot" that had the good fortune to slip through the bureaucratic net?

These questions can now, in part, be answered. The departmental archives contain a synopsis of the conversations between Atget and Vallery-Radot. These few lines summarize the photographer's life; they teach us nothing new, but they do offer the possibility that Atget might have existed as an individual in his interviewer's eyes and not just as a mere supplier. Molly Nesbit[2] has established that a privileged relationship did indeed exist between the photographer and the Bibliothèque: it was for the national library that he devised six

[1] This collection will be the subject of a publication in French by Marval in 2001.
[2] Nesbit, M., *Atget's Seven Albums*, New Haven/London: Yale University Press, 1992, p. 101.

Eugène Atget, *Parc de Saint-Cloud*, 1909-1911

albums of photographs, including the *Zoniers* and *Fortifications* mentioned above. Around 1924 he also provided a three-page handwritten list[3] of the 2,150 prints that complemented the collection of 2,600 negatives he had already sold to the Service des Beaux-Arts in 1920. The series of special interest to us is listed thus: "Park at St Cloud, Corners of the park: 132 prints, Cascade: 42 prints, In all: 174." One cannot avoid being struck by the note's laconic tone, given the beauty and variety of the images it describes.

These photographs were rediscovered in 1995[4] in an envelope annotated in Atget's own hand with the words: "Park at St Cloud. 111 prints. E. Atget. 17 *bis*, rue Campagne-Première (14e)." The group had been acquired for the sum of 333 francs, i.e. for 3 francs a picture, in July 1923, with the bookseller, and dealer in prints and photographs, Maurice Le Garrec, acting as middleman.

Whereas the other pictures in the series, depicting statues, balusters, terraces, and perspective views, were gathered together in a volume documenting the park at Saint-Cloud, this group of trees was too abstract and stayed in its original envelope, receiving no special treatment and stored in a box containing a less consulted series. At a time when, unlike prints, photographs were never classified under the artist's name, that they should be valued in the way we do today, was inconceivable. Their very acquisition, however, already amounted, if not to a gamble on the future, at least to a declaration of faith in the intrinsic worth of the images.

It transpires from a reading of the correspondence and the logbook of the departmental directors for the years 1900 to 1930 that, in their eyes, photography simply did not exist. They had a liking for Rembrandt, eighteenth-century engravings, and Dürer, for Corot, Delacroix, and Japanese prints, and these they approached in a competent and sensitive manner. The tens of thousands of photographs which were housed in the department, however, were considered neither positively nor negatively, were the subject of no discussion, attention, or curiosity — they were just nothing. Whether entering the collections through copyright deposit, deed of gift, or even purchase, photography remained invisible.

Perhaps one day we will discover that a few conservators, behind such institutional indifference, were indeed touched by a beauty which leaps out at us today. The most important thing, in the end, is that the accession, classification, and conservation of these rare works did indeed take place, and that they can be shown today for our delight.

SYLVIE AUBENAS
Conservateur en chef
Department of Prints and Photography
Bibliothèque Nationale de France

[3] Ibid., p. 202.
[4] By Luce Lebart, at the time a trainee with the Department.

Eugène Atget, *Parc de Saint-Cloud*, 1909-1911

50

Eugène Atget, *Parc de Saint-Cloud*, 1909-1911

Eugène Atget, *Parc de Saint-Cloud*, 1909-1911

Eugène Atget, *Parc de Saint-Cloud*, 1909-1911

53

Eugène Atget, *Parc de Saint-Cloud*, 1909-1911

Eugène Atget, *Parc de Saint-Cloud*, 1909-1911

55

Eugène Atget, *Cour* (Courtyard), *3, rue des Prouvaires*, 1913

Eugène Atget, *56, rue de la Verrerie*, s.d.

Eugène Atget, *90, rue Quincampoix*, s.d.

Eugène Atget, *18, quai de Béthune* • Eugène Atget, *Puits (The Well), 13, rue Sainte-Croix-de-la-Bretonnerie*, 1906
Eugène Atget, *6, rue Sauval*, 1907 • Eugène Atget, *12, rue Suger*, 1912

Eugène Atget, *Cour intérieure* (Interior Courtyard), ca 1912
Eugène Atget, *12, rue de la Parcheminerie*, 1912

Eugène Atget, *3, rue Sauval*, 1908

Eugène Atget, *Cour du Dragon* (The Dragon's Courtyard), 1913

Eugène Atget, *Quai de la Tournelle*, 1911

Eugène Atget, *Pont Neuf*, 1911

Eugène Atget, *63, quai de la Tournelle, "Au tambour"*, 1908

Eugène Atget, *Chez "E. Canet"*, 1901-1903 • Eugène Atget, *62, rue de l'Hôtel de Ville*, 1901-1903
Eugène Atget, *25, rue des Blancs-Manteaux, "À l'Homme armé"*, 1900 • Eugène Atget *1, quai de Bourbon, "Au franc Pinot"*, 1901-1902

Eugène Atget, 35, rue Geoffroy-Saint-Hilaire, "À la Biche", 1905 • Eugène Atget, 3, rue de l'Arbalète, marchand de vin (Wine Merchant), 1901
Eugène Atget, 54, rue Saint-André-des-Arts, "À la Croix d'Or", tabac (Tobacconist), 1900-1901 • Eugène Atget, 3, quai Conti, "Au petit Dunkerque", 1900

Eugène Atget, *6, rue de Jarente*, 1911

Jacques Darche, *Paris,* ca 1960

Eugène Atget, *Naturaliste* (Taxidermist), *rue de l'École-de-Médecine*, 1926

Jacques Darche, *Squelette en vitrine* (A Skeleton in a Shop Window), 1957

Eugène Atget, *Rue du Grenier-sur-l'Eau,* 1900-1901

Eugène Atget, *rue des Ursins*, s.d.

Eugène Atget, *Rue Rataud*, 1909

Eugène Atget, *Rue de Nevers*, 1924-1926

Eugène Atget, *Rue des Barres*, 1898

Eugène Atget, *Rue du Prévôt,* 1900-1901

Bill Brandt, *Snicket in Halifax*, 1948

Eugène Atget, *9, rue Thouin*, 1910

Bill Brandt, *Policeman in a Dockland Alley*, 1938

Eugène Atget, *Porte de Bercy. Gare du PLM* (PLM Railway Station), 1913

Jacques Darche, *Paris*, ca 1957

Eugène Atget, *Canal Saint-Denis*, 1925-27
Walker Evans, *Steel Mill (Aciérie). Burningham Alabama*, 1936

Eugène Atget, *Fortifications* (Fortifications), *Porte du Bas-Meudon*, 1907
Jacques Darche, *Arrêt "Cimetière"* (The "Cemetary" Bus Stop), 1957-1964

Eugène Atget, *Intérieur de M.B., collectionneur* (Interior of the Collector M.B.), *rue de Vaugirard*, 1910

Walker Evans, *Truro. Mass.*, 1931

Eugène Atget, *Intérieur de M.C., décorateur* (Interior of the Decorator M.C.), *rue de Montparnasse, 1910*

Eugène Atget, *Intérieur de M.B., collectionneur* (Interior of the Collector M.B.), *rue de Vaugirard*, 1910 • Eugène Atget, *Intérieur* (Interior), 1910
Eugène Atget, *Intérieur de M.A., industriel* (Interior of the Industrialist M.A.), *rue Lepic*, 1910 • Eugène Atget, *Intérieur d'un ouvrier* (A Workman's Room), 1910

Walker Evans, *Interior near Copake* (Intérieur près de Copake), *New York*, 1933 • Walker Evans, *Farmer's kitchen* (Cuisine de paysan), *Hale County, Alabama*, 1936
Walker Evans, *Farmer's kitchen* (Cuisine de paysan), *Hale County, Alabama*, 1936

Eugène Atget, *Intérieur de Mme C., modiste* (Interior of the Milliner, Miss C.), *place Saint-André-des-Arts*, 1910 • Eugène Atget, *Cuisine* (Kitchen), *rue Montaigne*, 1910

Walker Evans, *Biloxi, Mississippi*, 1944

August Sander, *Vernisseur* (Varnisher), *Cologne,* 1932

Eugène Atget, *Facteur* (Postman), 1899

Eugène Atget, *Mitron* (Baker's Assistant), 1899
Eugène Atget, *Marchand d'abat-jour* (Lamp Shade Seller), 1899 • Eugène Atget, *Boulanger* (Baker), 1899

August Sander, *Agent immobilier* (Real Estate Agent), *Cologne*, ca 1928 • August Sander, *Huissier exploitant* (Bailiff), *Cologne*, 1931
August Sander, *Le pianiste* (The Pianist), 1928

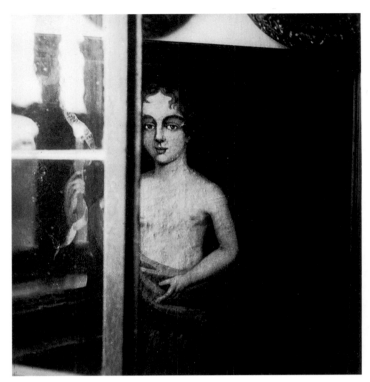

Jindrich Styrsky, 1934

Eugène Atget, *Magasin* (Shop), *avenue des Gobelins*, 1925

Eugène Atget, *Parc de Sceaux, mars 1925, 7 heures du matin* (March 1925, at 7 o'clock in the morning)

Lee Friedlander, *Central Park, New York*, 1994

Eugène Atget, *Square du Vert-Galant, Île-de-la-Cité*, 1899

Lee Friedlander, *George Washington Bridge, New Jersey*, 1973

Eugène Atget, *Porte de Bercy, sortie du PLM* (Exit of the PLM Station), *boulevard Poniatowski*, 1913

Eugène Atget, *Porte de Bercy, sortie du PLM* (Exit of the PLM Station), *boulevard Poniatowski*, 1913

Lee Friedlander, *Kansas City, Missouri*, 1965
Lee Friedlander, *Paris*, 1973

Jacques Darche, *Paris*, ca 1961
Jacques Darche, *Fontaine à Paris* (Fountain in Paris), 1957-1964

Eugène Atget, *41, rue Broca*, 1912

Walker Evans, *Stable* (Étable), *Natchez*, 1936

Eugène Atget, *Vieille cour* (Old Courtyard)*, 22, rue Saint-Sauveur*, 1914

Eugène Atget, *18, rue Sainte-Croix-de-la-Bretonnerie*, 1906 • Dieter Appelt, *Poutres, de la série "Transformed"* (Beams, from the Series "Transformed"), 1984

116

Eugène Atget, *25, rue des Francs-Bourgeois*, 1904

Eugène Atget, *Cour de la Monnaie, Quai Conti*, 1905-1906

Eugène Atget, *Cour (Courtyard), rue Visconti,* s.d.

119

Clarence John Laughlin, *Chicago, Poem in Shadow and Iron* (Poème d'ombre et de fer), 1962 • Eugène Atget, *"Au griffon", 39, rue de l'Horloge*, 1902

Eugène Atget, *15, rue de l'Ave-Maria*, s.d. • Clarence John Laughlin, *"The Brooding Wall"* ("Le mur des méditations"), 1965

Eugène Atget, *57, rue de Varenne, ambassade d'Autriche* (Austrian Embassy), 1905-1906

Eugène Atget, *Trianon*, 1923-1924

Clarence John Laughlin, *The translucent Triangle* (Triangle translucide), 1964

Eugène Atget, *Terme de Vertumne* (Boundary Statue of Vertumnus), *Parc de Sceaux, mai 1925, 7 heures du matin* (May 1925, at 7 o'clock in the morning)

Clarence John Laughlin, *"Elegy for the Moss Land"*, 1940

Vilem Kriz, *Buste dans un jardin de tulipes* (Bust in a Garden of Tulips), 1947

Eugène Atget, *Jardin de l'Hôtel de Cluny* (The Garden of the Hôtel de Cluny), 1912

129

Vilem Kriz, *Friche à Massy* (Fallow Land at Massy), 1949

Eugène Atget, *Fossé des fortifications à la Porte de Bercy* (Fortification Ditch at the Porte de Bercy), 1913

Vilem Kriz, *Entrée d'une vieille maison* (Entrance of an old House), 1946

Eugène Atget, *Cour de Rohan*, 1915

Vilem Kriz, *Rue à Paris* (A Street in Paris), 1950
Eugène Atget, *Rue Galande*, 15 avril 1899

134

Eugène Atget, *Bassin de la Villette* (Villette Dock), *quai de la Loire*, s.d.
Vilem Kriz, *Péniches au pont Alexandre III* (Barges at Alexandre III Bridge), 1948

Eugène Atget, *Rue du Petit-Thouars*, 1911

Eugène Atget, *Porte d'Asnières, Cité Trébert*, 1913

Eugène Atget, *La zone à la porte de Montreuil* (Slums at the Montreuil Gate), 1913

Eugène Atget, *Marché des Carmes, place Maubert*, 1911

Eugène Atget, *Fritures (Fryer), 38, rue de la Seine*, 1910

142

Eugène Atget, *Fritures (Fryer), Rue Mouffetard*, 1911

Albert Renger-Patzsch, 1928

Eugène Atget, *Marché des Carmes, Place Maubert*, 1911

Eugène Atget, *Foire du Trône* (The Fair of the "Throne"), 1925

Eugène Atget, *Boutique d'automobiles (Car Dealer), avenue de la Grande-Armée, 1924-1925*

Lee Friedlander, *Colorado,* 1967

Lee Friedlander, *Los Angeles*, 1965
Clarence John Laughlin, *"The Metaphysical Beauty Parlor. Or : What is real?"* ("Salon de beauté métaphysique ou Quelle réalité ?"), 1955

150

Eugène Atget, *"Spécialité de Toupet"* ("Specialized Wig Makers"), *Palais-Royal*, 1926-1927

Eugène Atget, *Porte du Pré-Saint-Gervais*, 1913

Eugène Atget, *Cheval d'omnibus* (Horse which pull the Bus), *église Saint-Médard*, 1901

153

Eugène Atget, *Rosier grimpant* (Climbing Rose), avant 1910 *(before 1910)*

Eugène Atget, *Tuileries*, 1921-1922

Lee Friedlander, *Pomona, New York,* 1977

Eugène Atget, *Luxembourg*, 1923-1926

Lee Friedlander, *Berkeley, California,* 1977

Eugène Atget, *Bagatelle, roseraie* (Rose Garden), 1921

Lee Friedlander, *Taos, New Mexico*, 1974

Eugène Atget, *6, rue de Palestine, Belleville*, 1901

Lee Friedlander, *Fort Lee, New Jersey,* 1975

163

Eugène Atget, *Square du Vert-Galant, Île-de-la-Cité*, 1911

Lee Friedlander, *East Chatham, New York,* 1974

Eugène Atget, *Vase au jardin des Tuileries* (Urn in the Tuileries Garden), 1911
Lee Friedlander, *Paris, 1972*

Eugène Atget, *Détail d'un vase au soleil par Drouilly* (Detail of an Urn by the Sculptor Drouilly), *Parc de Versailles*, s.d.

Eugène Atget, *Parc de Saint-Cloud*, 1922

Eugène Atget, *Parc de Saint-Cloud*, ca 1922-1923
Eugène Atget, *Parterre d'eau. Bassin du Nord.* (Expanse of Water. North Dock). *La Seine par Le Hongre,* s.d.

Eugène Atget, *Saint-Cloud*, 1915
Bruno Réquillart, *Versailles*, 1977

171

Bruno Réquillart, *Grand Canal, Versailles*, 1977

Eugène Atget, *Escalier du Grand Canal* (The Steps of the Grand Canal), *Grand Trianon, Versailles*, s.d.

Bruno Réquillart, *Versailles*, 1977

Eugène Atget, *Statue de la Servitude* (Statue of the Slavery), *parc de Sceaux, mars 1925, 8 heures du matin* (March 1925, at 8 o'clock in the morning)

Bruno Réquillart, *Les Cent Marches* (The Hundred Steps), *Versailles*, 1977

Eugène Atget, *Les Cent Marches* (The Hundred Steps), *Parc de Versailles*, 1901

Eugène Atget, *Fortifications* (Fortifications), *Porte Maillot*, 1913

179

Eugène Atget, *Fortifications* (Fortifications), *Porte Dauphine*, 1913

Lee Friedlander, *Washington DC*, 1973

Eugène Atget, *Porte Dauphine, Fossé des fortifications* (Fortification Ditch), 1913

Lee Friedlander, *Pomona, New York*, 1975

Eugène Atget, *Parc de Sceaux, L'Enlèvement de Proserpine* (The Rape of Proserpine), 1925

When the doctor who had come to sign Atget's death certificate asked his neighbors: "What did he die from?," they replied: "He was an eccentric." Atget's predominant characteristic throughout his life had been independence of mind. Though he held firm convictions and, when he felt the need, could express his opinions vehemently, he would avoid airing them. Never one to wear his heart on his sleeve, Atget shunned outside influences and was impatient of attempts to pigeonhole him. Those critics and historians of today who are disconcerted by Atget's reticence in respect of his art perhaps need look no further for an explanation. Atget lived at a time when it was possible for art to progress without its being dragged back by a mass of theory.

This discreetly private life was counterbalanced by Atget's abiding passion for the theater and a fondness for dramatic recitation. In order to hide one's innermost personality, nothing is more effective than playing a part.

"The mind only feels truly free in that state of security that comes from the intellect being perfectly honed" (Henri Focillon). Atget's life was lived out in accordance with the certainty offered by long-held inner truths; he asked for nothing more. Such a silence should be respected.

Atget was born into a family of artisans on February 12, 1857 at Libourne, a small town near Bordeaux dedicated to the wine trade. At the age of five he lost his parents and was brought up by his uncle. He did well in his classical education but then, for reasons which remain unknown, he became a sailor, seaman, or cabin boy on a sailing craft in the navy. The number and destinations of his various voyages are for the most part still uncertain. 1878 found Atget in Paris where he acquired a fervor for the theater. He took the very exacting competitive entrance examination to the Conservatoire, and, in spite of having a regional accent (considered a handicap at the time), was well received by the jury. Having failed the first time around, he passed at the second attempt. Eventually, however, he was forced to abandon his studies as they interfered with the current necessity of undertaking five years of military service. He embarked nonetheless on a career on the stage, joining a rather undistinguished troupe of traveling players. Whilst with them, he fell in love with the woman who was to share his life, Valentine Compagnon, herself of thespian stock.

She was to remain his companion for 40 years, although they never actually married. The woman, whom the neighbors were mindful of styling "Madame Atget," stood by him through thick and thin.

Of medium height with somewhat coarse features, Atget's was not a physique suited to playing the young lead and he had to make do with less prepossessing roles. After touring in the provinces as well as in Paris, Atget was forced to accept that he would never be a successful actor. Afflicted by an infection of the vocal chords — only a temporary ailment if his future neighbors are to be believed — he abandoned the stage and, aided by his colleague, André Calmettes, turned enthusiastically to painting. The scant evidence that survives does not allow us to be sure whether the simplicity of composition and broad brush result from boldness or awkwardness.

Painting, however, did not keep the wolf from the door and around 1888, during a sojourn in the Somme, Atget made up his mind to become a photographer. It was a trade he was to exercise with exemplary persistence.

Despite this change in direction, he never quite abandoned his earlier enthusiasm for the theater. In his rare moments of leisure, would devour books, especially those about theater. He also gave talks and lectures on classical and romantic drama, under the auspices of the working men's colleges. Although he never returned to the stage, he continued to practise his art: after the ritual of the family lunch, on vacation afternoons, he would lock himself away and loudly recite great speeches from the repertory. The scene is not perhaps as pathetic as it sounds — Atget was not a man prone to self-pity — it is likely that, in his innermost being, literature, painting, and his trade as a photographer combined to commune with beauty. We can only conjecture, as he left no record of his reasons.

On becoming a photographer, he hung up his sign: "Documents for artists." He never officially styled himself a "photographer," but "lecturer" or "author/publisher" instead — probably for tax purposes, and it was perhaps for the same reason that he never claimed any status as an "artist." Food for thought indeed.

The early days were hard. Working with an 18x24-centimeter view camera with bellows, he printed on nitrate paper from glass-plate negatives. At the time this piece of equipment, which weighed upwards of 35 lbs, was common; only by the 1920s would it have appeared archaic.

Atget would first study the topography and history of each area from a guidebook; then, bent beneath the massive box and tripod and carrying his plates, he would scour the length and breadth of Paris. We know that often arrived in Sceaux before eight o'clock, which meant that he would have had to catch a very early local train. Afterwards came all the work of printing and classifying negatives and prints, as well as his correspondence with customers. For customers there had to be. Prospects for solo photographers were seriously restricted since the major outlets, such as Giraudon, employed their photographers under contract. Atget, who had a fiercely independent streak, never joined such a firm yet managed over the years to carve out a fine reputation and acquire a quality clientele. On the one side, there were famous artists, as diverse as Luc-Olivier Merson and Detaille, or Dunoyer de Segonzac and Dignimont. On the other, there were some approachable and enlightened curators — at the Bibliothèque Historique of the City of Paris, at the Print Room of the Bibliothèque Nationale, or at the Musée Carnavalet, for example — who purchased complete collections and thus allowed him to make a reasonable living.

After Baron Haussmann had sliced straight through the very belly of the city with his boulevards, some worthy souls tried their best to save what little survived: a Commission du Vieux Paris being formed in 1898. Collectors were particularly keen on remnants from the Parisian past and would go to visit Atget to see for themselves the fruits of his patient labors, every one delighting in the tireless gentleman's high-minded dignity as well as in the sheer quality of his work.

From 1897, Atget devoted considerable time and method to putting his ever-increasing collections in order. He built up what became 13 main series and eight supplementary ones, extending his investigations to both the inner and the outer suburbs, classifying and reclassifying his albums in response to a different client or to a new-found subject. In the area of documentary photography, such careful analysis constitutes an aesthetic approach to the real. Little by little, however, Atget was to free himself from the constraints of pure documentary work. He returned to re-photograph sites from the same viewpoint but more restrictively framed, the centering more pronounced. He worked increasingly in winter or spring under lengthening shadows, in gardens à la française or in deserted parks. Sometimes, it is a melancholic romanticism that comes to the fore (e.g. at Sceaux), at other times the constructions are deliberately built up from dark areas in a manner that borders on abstraction. In both cases Atget sloughs off the shackles of the style of his fellow professionals. He even envisaged publishing whole series on very narrow subjects (such as Parisian interiors, or the vehicles of Paris), but he never succeeded in this.

From 1901, and above all in his great period, 1919–22 — as he began to amass the areas of shade (Saint-Cloud) and lengthen the line of cropping to create dreamy landscapes — Atget found himself in step with the art of his time, but without undermining the integrity of the real. Although forever silent on the matter, enough of his character has been revealed for us to be sure that he would have held his own personal opinions on Monet and on Cézanne. What these ideas may have been, however, we shall never know, since Atget took his secrets to the grave.

The War was a depressing period for Atget. His stepson, the child of his partner Valentine Compagnon, was killed at the very beginning of the hostilities, while his clientele shrunk to almost nothing. It was only in 1919 that he could return to taking pictures with the same frequency. His business was rescued by a large purchase of his works made on behalf of the Archives des Monuments Historiques. The remainder of his studio was saved after his death by the American photographer Berenice Abbott, aided by Julien Levy and in agreement with the executor of Atget's will, his lifelong friend André Calmettes. Unlike the photographer, Calmettes had met with success in the theater, but he never lost his admiration for Eugène Atget whom he called a "courageous, strong artist."

Atget died on August 4, 1927, never having recovered from the death of Compagnon the previous year. He had lost strength and was eating badly. He made a dramatic appearance to his neighbors on the landing of 17 *bis* Rue Campagne-Première and, with the cry: "I'm dying!," collapsed.

Though by his death his work had not received the acclaim he had hoped it might, his genius was eventually recognized by the avant-garde. A youthful Man Ray — a neighbor of his — bought a series of prints he had selected with an eagle eye. Some of these were published in *La Révolution surréaliste* in June 1926 — at Atget's insistence, without mention of his name. If Atget had lived on just a few more years, he would have found fame, whether he would have appreciated it or not. It would have been truly edifying to have seen how — and how ironically — the testy old man might have taken it all. Deep down, he was a libertarian and his political thinking was extremely left-wing, though he never joined a political party. The kind of man to cry "stuff the Police and the National Guard," he was also not adverse to fine phrases, being from the old school. He was perceived as unassuming. Would he have raised his thunderous voice against a new generation for whom showing off seemed to form part and parcel of creative daring, or would he have kept his cards close to his chest and remained silent, just like the best photographs?[1]

JEAN-CLAUDE LEMAGNY

[1] This text is based essentially on research by the much-missed Jean Leroy and by Maria Morris Hambourg, conservator at the Metropolitan Museum, New York.

Berenice ABBOTT
(1898–1991)
American

Perhaps best-known for her historic role in rediscovering and publishing Atget's work, Abbott was also an influential photographer in her own right. She was also the founder and a teacher of the photographic program of the New School for Social Research in New York from 1934 to 1958. Funded by the WPAs Federal Art Project she worked from 1935 to 1939 on *Changing New York*, a photographic documentation of the city, clearly inspired by Atget's series on Paris. In this, Abbott described her aims "to preserve for the future an accurate and faithful chronicle in photographs of the changing aspects of the worlds greatest metropolis … to produce an expressive result in which moving details must coincide with balance of design and significance of subject." The results show precisely this combination of documentary rigor and modernist aesthetic. Atget's vision of the capital of the nineteenth century, Paris, is reinterpreted in the context of a twentieth-century capital, New York. Sublime shots of soaring skyscrapers appear alongside the minutiae of an older world, horses and carts in the streets, and the overflowing curiosity cabinets of specialty store windows.

Dieter APPELT
(born in 1935)
German

A student of Heinz Hajek-Halke's, who was a pioneer of "subjective photography" as well as an opera singer, Dieter Appelt combined photography with Body art, taking photographs of himself in ritual situations evocative of imaginary religions and of death and resurrection. Fascinated by the density and stratification of matter and by the marks left on it by time, his projects have included covering himself in mud and disguising himself as a bird-man. In the series on rafters in a loft, Appelt acts as a pure observer of the massive structures built by an anonymous joiner, which thus appear as pieces of sculpture.

Atget treated much the same subject in his series on old staircases. There too, it is the density of the forms occupying the space that comes to the fore, though Atget's eye remains descriptive as it is concerned above all with documentation. Appelt's views are in greater close-up than Atget's, to the point that his forms become almost "abstract", a strange concept for images that so exalt the thickness and material nature of objects.

Bernd BECHER
(born in 1931)
German

Hilla BECHER
(born in 1934)
German

Married in 1961, they work together as independent photographers out of Düsseldorf. From 1974, they have been professors at the Staatliche Kunstakademie there, teaching many young photography artists.

Their work is dominated by the clarity and exactitude of a project, recording industrial (and for the most part anonymous) architecture without recourse to lighting effects or special perspectives. Their dispassionate approach has more in common with sculpture than architecture or even photography and results in images of uncanny grandeur.

Atget's photographs too increase notably in power when viewed at one remove from the way they have been customarily perceived — that is as records or memories — and we concentrate instead on the massive or even monumental solitude with which they invest their subjects.

Bill BRANDT
(1904–83)
British

Brought up in Germany and Switzerland before becoming a student of Man Ray in Paris, from 1929–30, he was profoundly affected by Atget's photographs.

Working for a variety of London magazines, Brandt's first book was *The English at Home* (1936), while his most famous offering, *Perspective of Nudes* (1961), tackles the problem of optical distortion in photography. A hallmark of his powerful style is its strong contrasts. His photographs appear haunted, as if the very fact of seeing was invested, for Brandt, with a frightening quality.

In Brandt's hands the deep gaps hewn out of the urban landscape of which Atget was so fond become like backdrops to a play awaiting the entrance of a figure such as Jack the Ripper.

Jacques DARCHE
(1920–65)
French

An illustrator and layout designer, Darche was a well-known figure in the book world, but the importance of his photographic oeuvre was little acknowledged. He would crisscross Paris taking pictures for his own pleasure, but died in an accident before ever seeing most of his images printed up.

Darche pressed the rigor of the typographer and page designer's eye into the service of photography, yet without neglecting humor and poetry. The vertical rhythms with which Darche punctuated his images recall a similar approach in Atget.

Marcel DUCHAMP
(1887–1968)
French

At first a hugely talented painter, Marcel Duchamp was always intrigued by a world that would go "beyond" art. For this reason, he was greatly interested in photography: either because he found in it a "beauty of indifference" freed from the pleasures of looking (what he called "aesthetics"), or else on the contrary when he would use non-realistic techniques such as photograms or Kirlian effects to create visual innovations.

Duchamp made us appreciate fully that in fact the most original act in art is not to "make" something but to "choose" it: the selection of an object is already an artistic gesture. The bottle-rack found in a market is a famous example of a "ready-made" that attracts our attention as "art" by being newly transported into the museum. Though still very much in evidence, its patent sculptural qualities are bracketed off to make us reflect only on the act of the artist in selecting it.

Some see this act as a blatant symbol of capitalism in that it simply appropriates the work of others. Picasso is alleged to have said of Duchamp that he "was a man who did some good pictures."

Walker EVANS
(1903–75)
American

Pursuing his studies at the Sorbonne in 1926, he conserved a singular admiration for French literature, especially for the prose of Gustave Flaubert. He seems to have become acquainted with Atget's photographic work shortly after returning to the United States and was deeply influenced by it. He worked in New York, as well as in the Deep South in 1935–37. From 1945 to 1965 he worked for *Fortune* magazine. His book, *American Photographs* (1962), marked a turning-point in photographic publishing.

With André Kertész, Walker Evans is to be considered as he who went furthest with respect to photography itself. His images attain a supreme balance between the aptness of the composition and the spontaneity of the real. Some of his series (masks, houses) foreshadow "conceptual" approaches such as that of the Bechers.

With Evans, as with Atget before him, confronting the plane of the subject head-on in its absolute simplicity, became a powerful mode of expression in its own right. Frontality, the degree zero of photography, is co-opted into the service of a veritable lyricism.

Lee FRIEDLANDER
(born 1934)
American

His talent came to the fore in the 1960s with a number of exhibitions and publications. He has been the recipient of several Guggenheim grants.

His work is typical of the "New Vision" that arose in the United States 40 years ago and is sometimes known as "Social Landscape," although his research is concerned above all with the image itself. Friedlander's intention has been to combine, with an extreme precision, the elements of the composition as they emerge from what might appear the anarchical space of the modern cityscape. But he also tackled natural landscape, during what amounted to a direct dialogue with Atget's earlier photographs of parks in France. In this aspect of his work, Friedlander attains the very summit of photographic poetry.

Juxtaposition, continuity, anastomosis in the two-dimensional photographic space, or lines and forms, which are in fact distant from one another in the third dimension, are all sources of wonder as much for Friedlander as they were for Atget.

Vilem KRIZ
(1921– 94)
American of Czech origin

A student of Jaromir Funke and František Drtikol in Prague, following World War II he spent time working in Paris. He left permanently for the United States in 1952 and, from 1964, started teaching in California.

Kriz thought of himself as an authentic Surrealist and was perhaps the purest representative of that tendency in photography. Quite out of step with American movements of his time, Kriz's work depends on an eye that transfigures the subject and on the extraordinary quality of his printing.

Between his Slav origins and his future in America, Kriz chose to live in Paris through which he adored wandering in search of his dreams.

Clarence John LAUGHLIN
(1905–85)
American

Self-taught photographer from Louisiana. He became a photographer in 1945 and worked for various official organizations. He also published books, assembling an enormous library of works of fantasy literature.

A visionary if ever there was one, Laughlin evoked and convoked other worlds, often by way of darkroom work, but also by straight photography. Every image was for him a poem, a place both of meditation and mystery.

The apparent connections between the free-spirited Surrealist Laughlin and the methodical and objective documentary photographer Atget give us a sense of the extent to which our subconscious obeys its own universal laws.

Albert RENGER-PATZSCH
(1897–1966)
German

Professional photographer and a professor at Essen. His book *Die Welt ist Schön* could well have been entitled *Die Dinge*, and epitomizes the Neue Sachlichkeit of the 1920s–30s. Many-faceted, it might be defined as an encounter between the object itself and abstraction. The spatial and haptic presence intensified to a maximum degree and the object perceived as concentrated on itself are combined with the sculptural purity of the artistic object considered as an artwork.

On occasion, Atget's unblinking gaze also isolates an object: seen as a document that stands alone it can be used by the artist/client as he thinks fit. In the face of the sheer presence of the visible, the diverse reasons lying behind the work of various artists of different countries and milieus evaporates.

Bruno RÉQUILLART
(born in 1947)
French

He studied advertising and discovered photography that seemed to offer a door to life after his school years.

He made a number of representative reports about 1970s social movements. Influenced by Conceptual art, between 1972 and 1973 he produced a series of "statements" (steel shutters, advertising hoardings, tree

trunks, etc.) and sequences on the urban environment. His career was much marked by Americans such as Robert Frank and Lee Friedlander before proceeding through various stages whose continuity was assured by his concentration on materials, as much as on structures, forms, and visual planes.

His work devoted to Versailles (1977), influenced by Atget, may be considered as the culmination of an investigation into the nature of spatial perception and its reproduction in two dimensions.

August SANDER
(1876–1964)
German

He first studied painting but became a photographer in 1898 after having also spent some time as a coal miner. He set himself up on his own account in 1904. In 1920, he embarked on a vast portrait of the German people, a substantial proportion of this panorama of "types" being lost during World War II. Sander also produced Rheinland landscapes and published two anthologies of portraits in 1929. His work was only rediscovered at the beginning of the 1950s. Sander has no equal in his depiction of subjects in their social or psychological setting, at once partially unconscious yet wholeheartedly embraced.

Comparing the types of genius associated with different countries is a perilous business, but Atget the Frenchman had his being in a happy-go-lucky country — with its picture postcards and gentle farces — whereas the German Sander had the feeling of being in a country that remained at once under the heel of its medieval severity and already in the grip of a tragic destiny.

Jindřich Štyrský
(1899–1942)
Czech

Painter, poet, and stage designer, Štyrský was self-taught in photography, using it to conjure up a world of dreams in which he could exist as an artist. In Paris between 1925 and 1928, he became extraordinarily receptive to the unconscious Rimbaudlike poetry of the city's store-signs and its deserted streets. Štyrský co-founded and remained the driving-force behind the Czech Surrealist group and held exhibitions in Prague, though he published little in his lifetime.

Atget was also sensitive to the uncanny familiarity of the single object, as it suddenly emerges as if from some parallel universe.

27 Eugène Atget, *Rampe, 13, galerie Vivienne*, 1906, Bibliothèque nationale de France, Est., Paris.
Bernd and Hilla Becher, *Tour de réfrigération*, 1967, artists' collection.

28 Eugène Atget, *Arc-boutant de l'église St Séverin*, 1902, Bibliothèque historique de la ville de Paris.

29 Bernd and Hilla Becher, *Haut-fourneau*, 1969, artists' collection.

30 Walker Evans, *Negro Church, South Carolina*, 1936, © Walker Evans Archive, The Metropolitan Museum of Art / private collection.

31 Eugène Atget, *"Au bon coin", 2, rue des Haudriettes*, 1908, Bibliothèque nationale de France, Est.

32 Eugène Atget, *Rampe, 269, rue St-Jacques*, 1905, Bibliothèque nationale de France, Est.

33 Eugène Atget, *Rampe, 21, rue du Cherche-Midi*, 1906, Bibliothèque historique de la ville de Paris.

34 Eugène Atget, *Grue au pont du Louvre*, n.d., Bibliothèque historique de la ville de Paris.

35 Albert Renger-Patzsch, *Grue géante, Hambourg*, 1929, Albert Renger-Patzsch Archiv — Ann and Jürgen Wilde, Zülpich.

36 Eugène Atget, *Jardin du Luxembourg. Bec de gaz*, n.d., Bibliothèque nationale de France, Est., Paris.

37 Albert Renger-Patzsch, *Lampadaire*, 1930, Albert Renger-Patzsch Archiv — Ann and Jürgen Wilde, Zülpich.

38 Marcel Duchamp, *Porte-bouteilles*, 1961, photo by Graydon Wood, 1998, Philadelphia Museum of Art: gift of Jacqueline, Paul and Pierre Matisse, in memory of their mother Alexina Duchamp.

39 Eugène Atget, *Rampe, 5, rue de Montmorency*, 1908, Bibliothèque historique de la ville de Paris.
Eugène Atget, *Rampe, 57, rue de Varennes*, Bibliothèque nationale de France, Est., Paris.

40 Eugène Atget, *38, quai de Bourbon, enseigne de Tabac*, 1901–02, Musée Carnavalet, Paris.

41 Walker Evans, *Tin Relic*, 1930, © Walker Evans Archive, The Metropolitan Museum of Art / private collection.

42 Eugène Atget, *Détail de la fontaine de la rue de Grenelle par Bouchardon*, 1907, Musée Carnavalet, Paris.

43 Walker Evans, *African Mask*, 1935, © Walker Evans Archive, The Metropolitan Museum of Art / collection of Marian and Benjamin A. Hill.

44 Eugène Atget, *Parc de Saint-Cloud*, between 1909 and 1911, Bibliothèque nationale de France, Est., Paris.
Eugène Atget, *Parc de Saint-Cloud*, between 1909 and 1911, Bibliothèque nationale de France, Est., Paris.

45 Eugène Atget, *Parc de Saint-Cloud*, between 1909 and 1911, Bibliothèque nationale de France, Est., Paris.

47 Eugène Atget, *Parc de Saint-Cloud*, between 1909 and 1911, Bibliothèque nationale de France, Est., Paris.

49 Eugène Atget, *Parc de Saint-Cloud*, between 1909 and 1911, Bibliothèque nationale de France, Est., Paris.

50 Eugène Atget, *Parc de Saint-Cloud*, between 1909 and 1911, Bibliothèque nationale de France, Est., Paris.

51 Eugène Atget, *Parc de Saint-Cloud*, between 1909 and 1911, Bibliothèque nationale de France, Est., Paris.

52 Eugène Atget, *Parc de Saint-Cloud*, between 1909 and 1911, Bibliothèque nationale de France, Est., Paris.
Eugène Atget, *Parc de Saint-Cloud*, between 1909 and 1911, Bibliothèque nationale de France, Est., Paris.

53 Eugène Atget, *Parc de Saint-Cloud*, between 1909 and 1911, Bibliothèque nationale de France, Est., Paris.
Eugène Atget, *Parc de Saint-Cloud*, between 1909 and 1911, Bibliothèque nationale de France, Est., Paris.

54 Eugène Atget, *Parc de Saint-Cloud*, between 1909 and 1911, coll. Bibliothèque nationale de France, Est., Paris.
Eugène Atget, *Parc de Saint-Cloud*, between 1909 and 1911, Bibliothèque nationale de France, Est., Paris.

55 Eugène Atget, *Parc de Saint-Cloud*, between 1909 and 1911, Bibliothèque nationale de France, Est., Paris.
Eugène Atget, *Parc de Saint-Cloud*, between 1909 and 1911, Bibliothèque nationale de France, Est., Paris.

57 Eugène Atget, *Cour, 3, rue des Prouvaires*, 1913, Bibliothèque nationale de France, Est., Paris.

58 Eugène Atget, *56, rue de la Verrerie*, n.d., Bibliothèque nationale de France, Est., Paris.

59 Eugène Atget, *90, rue Quincampoix*, n.d., Bibliothèque nationale de France, Est., Paris.

60 Eugène Atget, *18, quai de Béthune*, n.d., Bibliothèque nationale de France, Est., Paris.
Eugène Atget, *6, rue Sauval*, 1907, Bibliothèque nationale de France, Est., Paris.
Eugène Atget, *Puits, 13, rue Ste Croix de la Bretonnerie*, 1906, Bibliothèque historique de la ville de Paris.
Eugène Atget, *12 rue Suger*, 1912, Musée Carnavalet, Paris.

61 Eugène Atget, *Cour intérieure*, c. 1912, Bibliothèque historique de la ville de Paris.
Eugène Atget, *12 rue de la Parcheminerie*, 1912, Bibliothèque historique de la ville de Paris.

62 Eugène Atget, *3, rue Sauval*, 1908, Bibliothèque nationale de France, Est., Paris.

63 Eugène Atget, *Cour du dragon*, 1913, Bibliothèque nationale de France, Est., Paris.

64 Eugène Atget, *Quai de la Tournelle*, 1911, Bibliothèque historique de la ville de Paris.

65   Eugène Atget, *Pont Neuf*, 1911, Bibliothèque historique de la ville de Paris.

67   Eugène Atget, *"Au tambour", 63, quai de la Tournelle*, 1908, Bibliothèque nationale de France, Est., Paris.

68   Eugène Atget, *Chez "E. Canet"*, between 1901 and 1903, Bibliothèque nationale de France, Est., Paris.
Eugène Atget, *"A l'Homme armé", 25, rue des Blancs-Manteaux*, 1900, Bibliothèque nationale de France, Est., Paris.
Eugène Atget, *62, rue de l'Hôtel de Ville*, between 1901 and 1903, Bibliothèque nationale de France, Est., Paris.
Eugène Atget, *"Au franc Pinot", 1, quai de Bourbon*, 1901-1902, Bibliothèque nationale de France, Est., Paris.

69   Eugène Atget, *"A la Biche", 35, rue Geoffroy St-Hilaire*, 1905, Bibliothèque nationale de France, Est., Paris.
Eugène Atget, *3, rue de l'Arbalète, marchand de vin*, 1901, Bibliothèque nationale de France, Est., Paris.
Eugène Atget, *"A la Croix d'Or", 54, rue St-André des Arts, tabac*, 1900-1901, Bibliothèque nationale de France, Est., Paris.
Eugène Atget, *"Au petit Dunkerque", 3, quai Conti*, 1900, Bibliothèque nationale de France, Est., Paris.

70   Eugène Atget, *6, rue de Jarente*, 1911, Bibliothèque historique de la ville de Paris.

71   Jacques Darche, *Paris*, c. 1960, Bibliothèque nationale de France, Est., Paris.

72   Eugène Atget, *Naturaliste, rue de l'école de Médecine*, 1926, The Museum of Modern Art, New York. Purchase.

73   Jacques Darche, *Squelette en vitrine*, 1957, Bibliothèque nationale de France, Est., Paris.

74   Eugène Atget, *Rue du Grenier sur l'Eau*, 1900-1901, Bibliothèque nationale de France, Est., Paris.

75   Eugène Atget, *rue des Ursins*, Bibliothèque historique de la ville de Paris, Paris.

77   Eugène Atget, *Rue Rataud*, 1909, Musée Carnavalet, Paris.

78   Eugène Atget, *Rue de Nevers*, between 1924 and 1926, Bibliothèque nationale de France, Est., Paris.

79   Eugène Atget, *Rue des Barres*, 1898, Bibliothèque nationale de France, Est., Paris.

80   Eugène Atget, *Rue du Prévôt*, 1900–01, Bibliothèque nationale de France, Est., Paris.

81   Bill Brandt, *Snicket in Halifax*, 1948, The Bill Brandt Archive, London.

82   Eugène Atget, *9, rue Thouin*, 1910, Bibliothèque historique de la ville de Paris.

83   Bill Brandt, *Policeman in a Dockland Alley*, 1938, The Bill Brandt Archive, London.

84   Eugène Atget, *Porte de Bercy. Gare du P.L.M.*, 1913, Bibliothèque nationale de France, Est., Paris.

85   Jacques Darche, *Paris*, c. 1957, Bibliothèque nationale de France, Est., Paris.

86   Eugène Atget, *Canal Saint-Denis*, 1925–27, The Museum of Modern Art, New York. Abbott-Lévy Collection, partial gift of Shirley C. Burden.
Walker Evans, *Steel Mill. Burningham Alabama*, 1936, Bibliothèque nationale de France, Est., Paris.

87   Eugène Atget, *Fortifications, Porte du Bas-Meudon*, 1907, Musée Carnavalet, Paris.
Jacques Darche, *Arrêt "cimetière"*, between 1957 and 1964, Bibliothèque nationale de France, Est., Paris.

89   Eugène Atget, *Intérieur de M.B., collectionneur, rue de Vaugirard*, 1910, Bibliothèque historique de la ville de Paris.

90   Walker Evans, *Truro. Mass.*, 1931, Bibliothèque nationale de France, Est., Paris.

91   Eugène Atget, *Intérieur de M.C., décorateur, rue de Montparnasse*, 1910, Bibliothèque historique de la ville de Paris.

92   Eugène Atget, *Intérieur de M.B., collectionneur, rue de Vaugirard*, 1910, Bibliothèque historique de la ville de Paris.
Eugène Atget, *Intérieur*, 1910, Bibliothèque historique de la ville de Paris.
Eugène Atget, *Intérieur de M.A., industriel, rue Lepic*, 1910, Bibliothèque historique de la ville de Paris.
Eugène Atget, *Intérieur d'un ouvrier, rue de Romainville*, 1910, Bibliothèque historique de la ville de Paris.

93   Walker Evans, *Interior near Copake, New York*, 1933, © Walker Evans Archive, The Metropolitan Museum of Art / private collection.
Walker Evans, *Farmer's Kitchen, Hale County, Alabama*, 1936, © Walker Evans Archive, The Metropolitan Museum of Art / La Banque et Caisse d'Epargne de l'Etat, Luxemburg.
Walker Evans, *Farmer's kitchen, Hale County, Alabama*, 1936, © Walker Evans Archive, The Metropolitan Museum of Art / Galerie Baudoin Lebon, Paris.

94   Eugène Atget, *Intérieur de Mme C., modiste, place St André des Arts*, 1910, Bibliothèque historique de la ville de Paris.
Eugène Atget, *Cuisine, rue Montaigne*, 1910, Bibliothèque historique de la ville de Paris.

95   Walker Evans, *Biloxi, Mississippi*, 1944, © Walker Evans Archive, The Metropolitan Museum of Art / Sandra Alvarez de Toledo Collection, Paris.

96   August Sander, *Vernisseur, Cologne*, 1932, © Die Photographische Sammlung/SK Stiftung Kultur — August Sander Archiv, Cologne; ADAGP, Paris, 2000.

97   Eugène Atget, *Facteur*, 1899, Bibliothèque historique de la ville de Paris.

98   Eugène Atget, *Mitron*, 1899, Bibliothèque historique de la ville de Paris.
Eugène Atget, *Marchand d'abat-jour*, 1899, Bibliothèque historique de la ville de Paris.
Eugène Atget, *Boulanger*, 1899, Bibliothèque historique de la ville de Paris.

99   August Sander, *Agent immobilier, Cologne*, c. 1928, © Die Photographische Sammlung/SK Stiftung Kultur — August Sander Archiv, Cologne; ADAGP, Paris, 2000.
August Sander, *Huissier exploitant, Cologne*, 1931, © Die Photographische Sammlung/SK Stiftung Kultur — August Sander Archiv, Cologne; ADAGP, Paris, 2000.
August Sander, *Le pianiste*, 1928, © Die Photographische Sammlung/SK Stiftung Kultur — August Sander Archiv, Cologne; ADAGP, Paris, 2000.

100 Jindřich Štyrský, 1934, photothèque print from the collections of the Centre Georges Pompidou / Musée national d'art moderne, Paris.
Jindřich Štyrský, 1934, photothèque print from the collections of the Centre Georges Pompidou / Musée national d'art moderne, Paris.
Jindřich Štyrský, 1934, photothèque print from the collections of the Centre Georges Pompidou / Musée national d'art moderne, Paris.
Jindřich Štyrský, 1934, photothèque print from the collections of the Centre Georges Pompidou / Musée national d'art moderne, Paris.

101 Eugène Atget, *Magasin avenue des Gobelins*, 1925, new print from original in the Museum of Modern Art, New York.
Eugène Atget, *Magasin avenue des Gobelins*, 1925, new print from original in the Museum of Modern Art, New York.
Eugène Atget, *Magasin avenue des Gobelins*, 1925, new print from original in the Museum of Modern Art, New York.

103 Eugène Atget, *Parc de Sceaux, mars 1925, 7 h du matin*, The Museum of Modern Art, New York. Abbott-Lévy Collection, partial gift of Shirley C. Burden.

104 Lee Friedlander, *Central Park, New York*, 1994, courtesy Fraenkel Gallery, San Francisco.

105 Eugène Atget, *Square du Vert Galant, Île de la Cité*, 1899, Bibliothèque nationale de France, Est., Paris.

106 Lee Friedlander, *George Washington Bridge, New Jersey*, 1973, courtesy Fraenkel Gallery, San Francisco.

107 Eugène Atget, *Porte de Bercy, sortie du P.L.M., boulevard Poniatowski*, 1913, Bibliothèque nationale de France, Est., Paris.

109 Eugène Atget, *Porte de Bercy, sortie du P.L.M., boulevard Poniatowski*, 1913, Bibliothèque nationale de France, Est., Paris.

110 Lee Fiedlander, *Kansas City, Missouri*, 1965, courtesy Fraenkel Gallery, San Francisco.
Lee Friedlander, *Paris*, 1973, courtesy Fraenkel Gallery, San Francisco.

111 Jacques Darche, *Paris*, vers 1961, Bibliothèque nationale de France, Est., Paris.
Jacques Darche, *Fontaine à Paris*, between 1957 and 1964, Bibliothèque nationale de France, Est., Paris.

113 Eugène Atget, *41, rue Broca*, 1912, Musée Carnavalet, Paris.

114 Walker Evans, *Stable, Natchez*, 1936, Sandra Alvarez de Toledo, Paris.

115 Eugène Atget, *Vieille cour, 22, rue Saint-Sauveur*, 1914, Centre des monuments nationaux, Paris.

116 Eugène Atget, *18, rue Ste Croix de la Bretonnerie*, 1906, Musée Carnavalet, Paris.

116-117 Dieter Appelt, *Poutres, de la série " Transformed "*, 1984, Bibliothèque nationale de France, Est., Paris.

117 Eugène Atget, *25, rue des Francs-Bourgeois*, 1904, Musée Carnavalet, Paris.

118 Eugène Atget, *Cour de la Monnaie, Quai Conti*, 1905-1906, Bibliothèque historique de la ville de Paris.

119 Eugène Atget, *Cour rue Visconti*, n.d., Bibliothèque historique de la ville de Paris.

120 Clarence John Laughlin, *Chicago, Poem in Shadow and Iron*, 1962, © The Historic New Orleans Collection/Bibliothèque nationale de France, Est., Paris.
Eugène Atget, *"Au griffon", 39, rue de l'Horloge*, 1902, Bibliothèque historique de la ville de Paris.

121 Eugène Atget, *15, rue de l'Ave Maria*, n.d., © The Historic New Orleans Collection/Bibliothèque nationale de France, Est., Paris.
Clarence John Laughlin, *"The Brooding Wall"*, 1965, Bibliothèque nationale de France, Est., Paris.

123 Eugène Atget, *57, rue de Varenne, ambassade d'Autriche*, 1905-1906, Bibliothèque nationale de France, Est., Paris.

124 Eugène Atget, *Trianon*, 1923–24, The Museum of Modern Art, New York. Abott-Lévy Collection, partial gift of Shirley C. Burden.

125 Clarence John Laughlin, *The Translucent Triangle*, 1964, © The Historic New Orleans Collection/Bibliothèque nationale de France, Est., Paris.

126 Eugène Atget, *Terme de Vertumne, Parc de Sceaux, mai 1925, 7 h du matin*, Musée de l'Île-de-France, Château de Sceaux.

127 Clarence John Laughlin, *"Elegy for the Moss Land"*, 1940, © The Historic New Orleans Collection/Bibliothèque nationale de France, Est., Paris.

128 Vilem Kriz, *Buste dans un jardin de tulipes*, 1947, Bibliothèque nationale de France, Est., Paris.

129 Eugène Atget, *Jardin de l'Hôtel de Cluny*, 1912, Musée Carnavalet, Paris.

130 Vilem Kriz, *Friche à Massy*, 1949, Bibliothèque nationale de France, Est., Paris.

131 Eugène Atget, *Fossé des fortifications à la Porte de Bercy*, 1913, Musée Carnavalet, Paris.

132 Vilem Kriz, *Entrée d'une vieille maison*, 1946, Bibliothèque nationale de France, Est., Paris.

133 Eugène Atget, *Cour de Rohan*, 1915, Bibliothèque nationale de France, Est., Paris.

134 Vilem Kriz, *Rue à Paris*, 1950, Bibliothèque nationale de France, Est., Paris.
Eugène Atget, *Rue Galande*, 15 April 1899, Bibliothèque nationale de France, Est., Paris.

135 Eugène Atget, *Bassin de la Vilette, quai de la Loire*, n.d., Musée Carnavalet, Paris.
Vilem Kriz, *Péniches au pont Alexandre III*, 1948, Bibliothèque nationale de France, Est., Paris.

137 Eugène Atget, *Rue du Petit-Thouars*, 1911, Bibliothèque historique de la ville de Paris.

138 Eugène Atget, *Porte d'Asnières, Cité Trébert*, 1913, The Museum of Modern Art, New York. Purchase.

139 Eugène Atget, *La Zone à la porte de Montreuil*, 1913, Musée Carnavalet, Paris.

141 Eugène Atget, *Marché des Carmes, place Maubert*, 1911, Bibliothèque historique de la ville de Paris.

142 Eugène Atget, *Fritures, 38, rue de la Seine*, 1910, new print from original in the Museum of Modern Art, New York.

143 Eugène Atget, *Fritures, Rue Mouffetard*, 1911, Bibliothèque historique de la ville de Paris.

144 Albert Renger-Patzsch, 1928, Albert Renger-Patzsch Archiv - Ann and Jürgen Wilde, Zülpich.

145 Eugène Atget, *Marché des Carmes, Place Maubert*, 1911, Bibliothèque historique de la ville de Paris.

147 Eugène Atget, *Foire du Trône*, 1925, courtesy George Eastman House.

148 Eugène Atget, *Boutique d'automobiles, avenue de la Grande Armée*, 1924–25, new print from original in the Museum of Modern Art, New York.

149 Lee Friedlander, *Colorado*, 1967, courtesy Fraenkel Gallery, San Francisco.

150 Lee Friedlander, *Los Angeles*, 1965, courtesy Fraenkel Gallery, San Francisco.
Clarence John Laughlin, *"The Metaphysical Beauty Parlor. or: What is real?"*, 1955, © The Historic New Orleans Collection/Bibliothèque nationale de France, Est., Paris.

151 Eugène Atget, *"Spécialité de Toupet", Palais Royal*, 1926–27, new print from original in the Museum of Modern Art, New York.

152 Eugène Atget, *Porte du Pré St Gervais*, 1913, Bibliothèque nationale de France, Est., Paris.

153 Eugène Atget, *Cheval d'omnibus, Eglise St Médard*, 1901, Musée Carnavalet, Paris.

155 Eugène Atget, *Rosier grimpant*, before 1910, The Museum of Modern Art, New York. Abbott-Lévy Collection, partial gift of Shirley C. Burden.

156 Eugène Atget, *Tuileries*, 1921–22, The Museum of Modern Art, New York. Abbott-Lévy Collection, partial gift of Shirley C. Burden.

157 Lee Friedlander, *Pomona, New York*, 1977, courtesy Fraenkel Gallery, San Francisco.

158 Eugène Atget, *Luxembourg*, 1923–26, The Museum of Modern Art, New York. Purchase.

159 Lee Friedlander, *Berkeley, California*, 1977, courtesy Fraenkel Gallery, San Francisco.

160 Eugène Atget, *Bagatelle, roseraie*, 1921, The Museum of Modern Art, New York. Abbott-Lévy Collection, partial gift of Shirley C. Burden.

161 Lee Friedlander, *Taos, New Mexico*, 1974, courtesy Fraenkel Gallery, San Francisco.

162 Eugène Atget, *6, rue de Palestine, Belleville*, 1901, Musée Carnavalet, Paris.

163 Lee Friedlander, *Fort Lee, New Jersey*, 1975, courtesy Fraenkel Gallery, San Francisco.

164 Eugène Atget, *Square du Vert Galant, Île de la Cité*, 1911, Bibliothèque nationale de France, Est., Paris.

165 Lee Friedlander, *East Chatham, New York*, 1974, courtesy Fraenkel Gallery, San Francisco.

167 Eugène Atget, *Vase au jardin des Tuileries*, 1911, Bibliothèque historique de la ville de Paris.
Lee Friedlander, *Paris*, 1972, courtesy Fraenkel Gallery, San Francisco.

168 Eugène Atget, *Détail d'un vase au soleil par Drouilly, Parc de Versailles*, Musée de l'Île-de-France, Château de Sceaux.

169 Eugène Atget, *Parc de Saint-Cloud*, August 1922, Bibliothèque nationale de France, Est., Paris.

170 Eugène Atget, *Parc de Saint-Cloud*, c. 1922–23, Bibliothèque nationale de France, Est., Paris.
Eugène Atget, *Parterre d'eau. Bassin du Nord. La Seine par Le Hongre*, n.d., Musée de l'Île-de-France, Château de Sceaux.

171 Eugène Atget, *Saint-Cloud*, 1915–19, Centre des monuments nationaux.
Bruno Réquillart, *Versailles*, 1977, © Ministère de la Culture - France.

172 Bruno Réquillart, *Grand Canal, Versailles*, 1977, © Ministère de la Culture - France.

173 Eugène Atget, *Escalier du Grand Canal, Grand Trianon, Versailles*, n.d., Musée de l'Île-de-France, Château de Sceaux.

174 Bruno Réquillart, *Versailles*, 1977, © Ministère de la Culture, France.

175 Eugène Atget, *Statue de la Servitude, Parc de Sceaux, mars 1925, 8 h du matin*, Musée de l'Île-de-France, Château de Sceaux.

176 Bruno Réquillart, *Les Cent Marches, Versailles*, 1977, © Ministère de la Culture, France.

177 Eugène Atget, *Les Cent Marches, Parc de Versailles*, 1901, Musée de l'Île-de-France, Château de Sceaux.

179 Eugène Atget, *Fortifications, Porte Maillot*, 1913, Musée Carnavalet, Paris.

180 Eugène Atget, *Fortifications, Porte Dauphine*, 1913, Musée Carnavalet, Paris.

181 Lee Friedlander, *Washington DC*, 1973, courtesy Fraenkel Gallery, San Francisco.

182 Eugène Atget, *Porte Dauphine, Fossé des fortifications*, 1913, Bibliothèque nationale de France, Est., Paris

183 Lee Friedlander, *Pomona, New York*, 1975, courtesy Fraenkel Gallery, San Francisco.

184 Eugène Atget, *Sceaux. Parc. L'Enlèvement de Proserpine*, 1925, Musée de l'Île-de-France, Château de Sceaux.

1929 Berenice Abbott, "Eugène Atget," in *Creative Art*, vol. 5, no. 3, September 1929, pp. 651–56.

1931 Walker Evans, "The Reappearance of Photography," in *Hound and Horn*, no. 1, October–December 1931, pp. 126–28.
Ansel Adams, "Photography," in *Fortnightly*, no. 5, November 1931, p. 25.

1936 Berenice Abbott, "Photographer as artist," in *Art Front*, September–October 1936, pp. 4–7.

1939 Manuel Alvarez-Bravo, "Adget [sic], Documentos para artista," in *Artes plastica*, no. 3, autumn 1939, pp. 68–76, 78.

1940 Berenice Abbott, "Eugène Atget, Forerunner of Modern Photography," in *US Camera*, vol. 1, no. 12, fall 1940, pp. 20–23, 48–49, 76; and no. 13, winter 1940, pp. 68–71.

1941 Berenice Abbott, "Paris in the Early 1900s," in *Harper's Bazaar*, no. 2750, April 1941, pp. 74–75.

1945 Berenice Abbott, "Atget, photographer of Paris," in *Minicam Photography*, no. 7, April 1945, pp. 36–41, 95.

1951 Berenice Abbott, "Eugène Atget," in *Complete Photographer*, no. 6, 1951, pp. 335–39.

1956 Minor White, "Eugène Atget, 1856–1927," [sic] in *Image*, no. 4, April 1956, pp. 76–83.
Berenice Abbott, *20 Photographs by Eugène Atget*, portfolio.

1963 Berenice Abbott, *Eugène Atget*, Prague.

1964 Berenice Abbott, *The World of Atget*, Horizon Press, New York (reprint: Paragon Books, New York, Puttmans' Sons, 1979); including 176 photographs.

1966 Edward Weston, "Daybooks, December, 27, 1930," in *The Daybooks of Edward Weston*, volume III, Horizon Press with the George Eastman House, New York and Rochester.

1969 Brassaï, Gyula Halász, "My Memories of Eugène Atget, P. H. Emerson and Alfred Stieglitz," in *Camera*, vol. 48, no. 1, January 1969, pp. 4–13, 21, 27, 37.

1975 Paul Hill and Tom Cooper, "Interview Man Ray," *Camera*, vol. 54, no. 2, February 1975, pp. 37–40.

1986 Robert Doisneau, "Atget, je peux vous poser une question !" in *Colloque Atget, Photographies*, special issue, 1986, pp. 100–04.
Holger Trülzsch, "Atget Minotaure," in *Colloque Atget, Photographies*, special issue, March 1986, pp. 30–37.

1989 Robert Doisneau, "Monsieur Atget à la Poterne des Peupliers," in *À l'imparfait de l'objectif, Souvenirs et Portraits*, Pierre Belfond, Paris.

1926   *La Révolution surréaliste*, no. 7, June 15, 1926, (reproductions of photographs by Atget on the cover and pp. 6, 28).
La Révolution surréaliste, no. 8, December 1, 1926 (reproduction of a photograph by Atget on p. 20).

1928   Florent Fels, "Le premier Salon indépendant de la photographie," in *L'Art Vivant*, no. 4, June 1, 1928, p. 445.
Pierre Bost, "Premier Salon indépendant de la photographie," in *La Revue Hebdomadaire*, no. 24, June 1928, pp. 356–59.
Robert Desnos, "Eugène Atget," in *Le Soir*, 11 September 1928, p. 6.
Pierre Mac Orlan, "La photographie et le fantastique social," in *Les Annales*, no. 2321, November 1, 1928, pp. 413–14.
Eugène Valentin, "Eugène Atget (1856-1927)," in *Variétés*, no. 8, December 15, 1928, pp. 403–07.
Roger Vaillant, "Un homme qui fit en trente ans dix mille photographies de Paris," in *Paris-Midi*, 26 October 1928.

1929   Jean Galloti, "Atget," in *L'Art vivant*, January 1, 1929, pp. 20–21, 24.
Robert Desnos, "Émile Adget," [sic], in *Merle*, new series, no. 3, May 3, 1929 (reprinted in *Nouvelles-Hébrides et autres textes, 1922-1930*, Gallimard, Paris, 1978, pp. 435ff.).
Janet Flanner, "Eugène Atget (1856-1927)," in *The New Yorker*, May 4, 1929, p. 79 (reprinted in *Paris Was Yesterday (1925–1939)*, Popular Library, New York, 1972).
Berenice Abbott, "Eugène Atget," in *Creative Art*, vol. 5, no. 3, September 1929, pp. 651–56.
Film und Foto, catalogue, Stuttgart, 1929 (reproduction of 10 photos by Atget).

1930   Waldemar George, "Photographie vision du monde, Adget [sic] photographe de Paris," in *Arts et métiers graphiques*, no 16, March 15, 1930, pp. 134–38.
Atget photographe de Paris, preface by Pierre Mac Orlan, Paris, Jonquières (American edition, New York, Weyhe; German edition, *Eugène Atget. Lichtbilder*, preface by Camille Recht, Paris and Leipzig). 96 photographs.

1931   Paul Rosenfeld, "Paris, the artist," in *The New Republic*, no. 843, January 28, 1931, pp. 299–300.
Florent Fels, "L'Art photographique. Adget," [sic] in *L'Art vivant*, no. 145, February 1931, p. 28.
Walker Evans, "The Reappearance of Photography," *Hound and Horn*, no. 1, October–December 1931, pp. 126–28.

Ansel Adams, "Photography," in *Fortnightly*, no. 5, November 6, 1931, p. 25.
Walter Benjamin, "A Short History of Photography" in *One-Way Street and Other Writings*, London, 1979.

1936   Berenice Abbott, "Photographer as artist," in *Art Front*, September–October 1936, pp. 4–7.

1939   Kospoth B.-J., "Eugène Atget," in *Transition*, no. 15, February 1939, pp. 122–24.
Pierre Mac Orlan, "Atget," in *L'Art vivant*, no. 230, March 1939, p. 48.
Manuel Alvarez-Bravo, "Adget [sic], Documentos para artista," in *Artes plastica*, no. 3, fall 1939, pp. 68–76, 78.

1940   Berenice Abbott, "Eugène Atget, Forerunner of Modern Photography," in *US Camera*, vol. 1, no. 12, fall 1940, pp. 20–23, 48–49, 76 and no. 13, winter 1940, pp. 68–71.

1941   Berenice Abbott, "Paris in the Early 1900s," in *Harper's Bazaar*, no. 2750, April 1941, pp. 74–75.
Photographie ancienne, no. 23.

1945   Berenice Abbott, "Atget, photographer of Paris," *Minicam Photography*, no. 7, April 1945, pp. 36–41, 95.

1951   Berenice Abbott, "Eugène Atget," in *Complete Photographer*, no. 6, 1951, pp. 335–39.
Yvan Christ, *Saint-Germain-des-Prés 1900 vu par Atget*, Comité de la quinzaine de Saint-Germain, Paris, 1951.

1956   Minor White, "Eugène Atget, 1856–1927," [sic] in *Image*, no. 4, April 1956, pp. 76–83.
Berenice Abbott, *20 Photographs by Eugène Atget*, portfolio.

1962   Jean Leroy, "Eugène Atget qui étiez-vous?" in *Camera*, vol. 41, no. 12, December. 1962, pp. 6–8 (reprinted in *Camera*, vol. 57, no. 3, March 1978).

1963   Berenice Abbott, *Eugène Atget*, Prague.
Paris du temps perdu : photographies d'Eugène Atget, texts by Marcel Proust, Edita, Lausanne, Bibliothèque des arts, Paris.

1964   Clement Greenberg, "Four photographs," in *New York Review of Books*, no. 11, January 1964, pp. 8–9.
Berenice Abbott, *The World of Atget*, Horizon Press, New York (new edition by Paragon Books, Puttmans' Sons, New York, 1979). 176 photographs.
Jean Leroy, "Atget et son temps," in *Terre d'images*, no. 3, May 1964.

1968   John Fraser, "Atget and the City," in *Cambridge Quarterly*, no. 3, pp. 199–233.

1969   Brassaï, Gyula Halász, "My Memories of Eugène Atget, P. H. Emerson and Alfred Stieglitz," in *Camera*, vol. 48, no. 1, January 1969, pp. 4–13, 21, 27, 37.

1971   Yvan Christ, *Le Paris d'Atget*, Balland.

1974 Jean-Claude Lemagny, "Le bonhomme Atget," in *Photo*, no. 87, December 1974.

1975 Jean Leroy, *Atget, magicien du vieux Paris*, Pierre-Jean Balbo, Joinville-le-Pont.
Paul Hill and Tom Cooper, "Interview Man Ray," in *Camera*, vol. 54, no. 2, February 1975, pp. 37–40.
John Szarkowski, "Atget's Trees," in *One Hundred Years of Photographic History: Essays in Honor of Beaumont Newhall*, Van Deren Coke, Albuquerque, University of New Mexico, pp. 161–68.

1976 Molly Nesbit, "Atget's Book *L'art dans le vieux Paris*. Tradition and the Individual Photographic Talent," Yale University Press, New Haven.

1977 John Fuller, "Atget and Man Ray in the Context of Surrealism," in *Art Journal*, no. 2, winter 1976–77, pp. 130–38.
Jean Leroy, "Photojournal : précisions sur Atget," in *Photos*, special issue, November 1977, p. 15.
Julien Levy, "Atget," in *Memoir of an Art Gallery*, Puttman's Sons, New York, 1977, pp. 90–95.
William Johnson, "Eugène Atget. A Chronological Bibliography," in *Exposure*, May 1977.

1978 Jean Leroy, "Eugène Atget qui étiez-vous ?" in *Camera*, vol. 57, no. 3, March 1978. pp. 40–42 (reprinted in *Camera*, vol. 41, no. 12, December 1962, pp. 6–8).
Alain Pougetoux and Romeo Martinez, *Eugène Atget photographe 1857-1927*, Paris, Musées de France.

1979 Jean Leroy, "La vérité sur Atget," in *Camera*, vol. 58, no. 11, November 1979, pp. 15, 41–42.
Atget : voyages en ville, texts by Romeo Martinez and Alain Pougetoux, introduction by Pierre Gassmann, Chêne-Hachette, Paris.
Atget's Gardens, a Selection of Eugène Atget's Photographs, text by William Howard Adams, London (RIBA), New York (ICP), Washington (IEF). 77 photographs.
Barbara Michaels, "An Introduction to the Dating and Organization of Eugène Atget's Photographs," in *Art Bulletin*, vol. 6, no. 3, pp. 460–68.

1980 Hans Georg Puttnies, *Atget*, catalogue by the Rudolf Kicken Gallery, Cologne.
Berenice Abbott, *The World of Atget*, New York, Horizon Press.

1981–85 John Szarkowski and Maria Morris Hambourg, *The Work of Atget*, 4 volumes published by MoMA, New York:
Vol. 1 (1981), *Old France*, 121 plates and 83 small reproductions, "Atget and the Art of Photography" by John Szarkowski, entries by Maria Morris Hambourg;
Vol. 2 (1982), *The Art of Old Paris*, 117 plates and 95 small reproductions, "A Biography of Eugène Atget" and entries by Maria Morris Hambourg;
Vol. 3 (1983), *The Ancien Régime*, 120 plates and 47 small reproductions, "The Structure of the Work" by Maria Morris Hambourg, entries by John Szarkowski;
Vol. 4 (1985), *Modern Times*, 116 plates and 86 small reproductions, "Understandings of Atget" and entries by John Szarkowski.

1982 Margaret Nesbit and Françoise Reynaud, *Eugène Atget, Intérieurs parisiens artistiques, pittoresques et bourgeois, début XXᵉ siècle*, an album by the Musée Carnavalet, Carré and Paris-Musées, Paris.
Claire Fons, *Quand Atget photographiait Rouen*, Rouen CRDP.
Rosalind Krauss, "Photography's Discursive Spaces: Landscape/View," in *Art Journal*, no. 41, 1982. pp. 311–19.

Roberta Hellman, Marvin Hoshimo, "On the Rationalisation of Eugène Atget," in *Arts Magazine*, February 1982.

1983 Gerry Badger, "Atget and the Garden of Critical Delights," in *The Photographic Collector*, vol. 3, no. 1, spring 1983, pp. 41–43.

1984 James Borcoman, *Eugène Atget*, National Gallery of Canada, Ottawa.
Françoise Reynaud, *Eugène Atget*, photopoche no. 16, Centre national de la photographie, Paris.
Maria Morris Hambourg, "Atget, Precursor of Modern Documentary photography," in *Untitled*, no. 35, The Friends of Photography, Carmel, 1984, pp. 24–39.

1985 Gerry Badger, *Eugène Atget*, Masters of Photography series, Macdonald, London.
Françoise Raynaud, *Eugène Atget: a Selection of Photographs from the Collection of the Musée Carnavalet, Paris*, Pantheon, New York.

1986 "Colloque Atget, actes du colloque tenu au Collège de France, 14 au 15 juin 1985," in *Photographies*, special issue, March 1986.

1987 Max Kozloff, "Abandoned and Seductive: Atget's Streets," in *The Privileged Eye*, Albuquerque, University of New Mexico Press, pp. 279–304.

1988 *Paris vu par Atget et Cartier-Bresson*, Tokyo Metropolitan Foundation, Tokyo.

1990 *Regards sur Versailles : Photographies d'Eugène Atget, André Ostier, Maryvonne Gilotte et Paul Maurer*, Musée Lambinet, Versailles.

1991 *Les Hauts-de-Seine en 1900. 127 photographies d'Eugène Atget*, catalogue published by the conseil général des Hauts-de-Seine.
Françoise Reynaud, *Les voitures d'Atget au musée Carnavalet*, Carré and Paris-Musées, Paris.

1992 Molly Nesbit, *Atget's Seven Albums*, Yale University Press, New Haven and London.
Jean Leroy, *Atget, magicien du vieux Paris*, P.-J. Balbo, Joinville-le-Pont (second edition).

1993 Dominique Baqué, "À l'origine du modernisme, Atget," in *Les Documents de la modernité, anthologie de textes sur la photographie de 1919 à 1939*, pp. 398–412.
Laure Beaumont-Maillet, *Atget's Paris*, Thames and Hudson, London.

1994 Molly Nesbit, "Eugène Atget, le photographe et l'histoire," in *Nouvelle histoire de la photographie* edited by Michel Frizot, Adam Biro and Bordas, Paris.
Buisine Alain, *Eugène Atget ou la mélancolie en photographie*, Jacqueline Chambon, Nîmes.
Olivier Lugon, *Le "Style documentaire" dans la photographie allemande et américaine des années vingt et trente*, doctoral thesis under the direction of Pierre Vaisse, University of Geneva.

1997 Daniel Quesney, "L'intuition des photographes," in *Séquences paysages*, journal of the Observatoire photographique du paysage, no. 1, 1997.

1998 Guilaume Le Gall, *Atget Paris pittoresque*, Hazan, Paris.
Eugène Atget. A Retrospective. An Intimate View of Paris at the Turn of the Century, Tokyo Metropolitan Museum of Photography.
Wilfried Wiegand, *Eugène Atget, Paris*, Schirmer-Mosel, Munich.

1999 David Harris, *Eugène Atget. Itinéraires parisiens*, Musée Carnavalet, Éditions du Patrimoine and Paris-Musées, Paris.

2000 Guillaume Le Gall, "Atget, figure réfléchie du surréalisme," in *Études photographiques*, no. 7, May 2000, pp. 90–107.

Abbott, Berenice 7, 8, 9, 15, 16, 20, 21, 22, 23, 24, 48, 186, 187
Adams, Ansel 8, 21
Addison Gallery of American Art 9
Agha, M.-F. 8, 23
Albright Art Gallery 22
Alvarez-Bravo, Manuel 9, 22
American Monument, The 8
American Photographs 23, 188
Appelt, Dieter 3, 17, **116**, 187
Après-midi à Paris 8
Aragon, Louis 19
Archives des Monuments historiques 186
Archives photographiques 20, 23
Arp, Jean 19
Artaud, Antonin 19
Art dans le vieux Paris, L' 20
Atget, Eugène 7, 8, 9, 10, 11, 12, 13, 14, 15, 16, 17, 18, 19, 20, 21,
    22, 23, 24, **27**, **28**, **30**, **31**, **32**, **33**, **34**, **36**, **39**, **40**, **42**, **44**, **45**, **47**,
    48, 49, **49**, **50**, **51**, **52**, **53**, **54**, **55**, **57**, **58**, **59**, **60**, **61**, **62**, **63**, **64**,
    65, **67**, **68**, **69**, **70**, **72**, **74**, **75**, **77**, **78**, **79**, **80**, **82**, **84**, **86**, **87**, **89**,
    91, **92**, **94**, **97**, **98**, **101**, **103**, **105**, **107**, **109**, **113**, **115**, **116**, **117**,
    118, **119**, **120**, **121**, **123**, **124**, **126**, **129**, **131**, **133**, **134**, **135**,
    137, **138**, **139**, **141**, **142**, **143**, **145**, **147**, **148**, **151**, **152**, **153**,
    155, **156**, **158**, **160**, **162**, **164**, **167**, **168**, **169**, **170**, **171**, **173**,
    175, **177**, **179**, **180**, **182**, **184**, 185, 186, 187, 188, 189
Atget photographe de Paris 8, 20
Barbin, Pierre 9
Beaux-Arts, Écoles des 3, 49, 186, 187
Becher, Bernd and Hilla 3, 8, 13, 16, 23, **27**, **29**, 187, 188
Bellmer, Hans 20
Benjamin, Walter 3, 8, 9, 20, 21
Bibliothèque historique de la Ville de Paris 3, 7, 186
Bibliothèque nationale 2, 3, 7, 17, 48, 186
Bifur 20
Bovis, Marcel 8
Brady, Mathew B. 22
Brandt, Bill 3, 8, 9, 15, **81**, **83**, 187
Braque, Georges 16
Brassaï 22, 23, 24
Calmettes, André 8, 9, 20, 24, 185, 186
Cartier-Bresson, Henri 22
Cézanne, Paul 186
Changing New York 20, 21, 22
Charlot, Jean 8
Cherronnet, Louis 23
Chevrier, Jean-François 9
Chicago Tribune 8
Christ, Yvan 9
Collège de France 7, 9, 19, 23
Comédie des Champs-Élysées 8

Commission du Vieux Paris 186
Commune 14
Compagnon, Valentine 7, 9, 185, 186
Corot, Jean-Baptiste Camille 49
Crapouillot, Le 8
Creative Art 8, 21
Crevel, René 19
Dalí, Salvador 19
Darche, Jacques 3, 17, **71**, **73**, **85**, **87**, **111**, 187
Daybooks 8
De Chirico, Giorgio 19, 20
Delacroix, Eugène 49
Demachy, Robert 2, 20
Derain, André 7
Desnos, Robert 8, 19
Detaille, Édouard 186
Die Welt ist Schön 189
Dignimont 186
Doisneau, Robert 8, 23, 24
Donatello 17
Douanier Rousseau, le 19, 23
Drtikol, František 188
Du Camp, Maxime 48
Dubreuil, Pierre 12
Duchamp, Marcel 11, 13, 16, **38**, 188
Dunoyer de Segonzac, André 7, 186
Dürer, Albrecht 49
El Greco 17
Essen 189
Études photographiques 8, 20
Evans, Walker 9, 10, 14, 15, 17, 19, 21, 22, 23, 24, **30**, **41**, **43**, **86**,
    90, **93**, **95**, **114**, 188
Fels, Florent 8
Fierens, Paul 21
FIFO 20, 21, 22
Film und Foto 8, 20, 21
Flaubert, Gustave 24, 188
Flowers and Trees 8
Focillon, Henri 185
Foire du Trône **147**
Fortnightly, The 8, 21
Fortune 188
Foto-Auge 21, 22
Fotografie der Gegenwart 21
Foujita, Léonard 7
France travaille, La 20
Frank, Robert 22, 189
Fraser, John 9
Friedlander, Lee 3, 8, 9, 17, 22, 23, **104**, **106**, **110**, **149**, **150**, **157**,
    159, **161**, **163**, **165**, **167**, **181**, **183**, 188, 189

Frizot, Michel 9
Funke, Jaromir 188
Galerie L'Époque 21
Galerie Vivienne 27
George, Waldemar 3, 8, 9, 19, 21, 22
Germany 8, 21, 23, 24, 187
Gibson, Ralph 16
Giraudon 186
Got, Edmond 7
Grand Trianon **173**
Greenberg, Clement 9
Hambourg, Maria Morris 9, 186
Harris, David 9
Harvard 22
Haussmann, baron Georges 9, 14, 186
Heidegger, Martin 12
Hill, Paul 19, 22, 23
Hound and Horn 8, 21
Hugo, Victor 11, 14, 15
Intérieurs parisiens artistiques, pittoresques et bourgeois 23
Izis 24
Jammes, André 7, 23
Jonquières 20, 23
Kant, Emmanuel 15
Katz, Leslie 9, 22, 23
Kenna, Michael 9
Kertész, André 8, 20, 21, 22, 23, 188
Kirstein, Lincoln 22, 23
Kisling, Moïse 7
Kollar, François 20
Kriz, Vilem 3, 9, 17, **128**, **130**, **132**, **134**, **135**, 188
Krull, Germaine 8, 21
Labiche, Eugène 189
Lartigue, Jacques-Henri 7
Laughlin, Clarence John 9, 17, 22, **120**, **121**, **125**, **127**, **150**, 189
Le Garrec, Maurice 48, 49
Le Gray, Gustave 15
Leiris, Michel 19
Lemagny, Jean-Claude 2, 5, 9, 17, 186
Leroy, Jean 9, 23, 186
Lévi-Strauss, Claude 15
Levy, Julien 8, 22, 186
Lipchitz, Jacques 16
Lugon, Olivier 20, 21, 22, 23
Mac Orlan, Pierre 8, 20, 23
Man Ray 7, 8, 11, 19, 20, 21, 22, 23, 24, 48, 186, 187
Manet, Édouard 17
Martinez, Romeo 9
Marville 12, 14, 23
Merson, Luc-Olivier 186
Meryon, Charles 15
Metropolitan Museum of Art, New York 3, 16, 186
Minotaure, Le 19, 20
MoMA, New York 8, 9, 20, 22, 23
Monet, Claude 186
Musée Carnavalet 3, 7, 9, 23, 24, 186
Musée des Arts décoratifs 3, 23
Nadar 8, 21, 22
Nerval, Gérard de 14
Nesbit, Molly 9
New York 2, 3, 8, 9, 16, 20, 21, 22, 23, 93, **104**, **157**, **165**, **183**, 186, 188
Nietzsche, Friedrich 25
New Objectivity 8, 21, 189
Outerbridge, Paul 8, 21
Paris 2, 3, 7, 8, 9, 14, 15, 16, 17, 19, 20, 21, 22, 23, 24, 48, **71**, **85**, **110**, **111**, **134**, **167**, 185, 186, 187, 188, 189

pont Alexandre III **135**
rue de l'Arbalète **69**
porte d'Asnières **138**
rue de l'Ave-Maria **121**
Bagatelle **160**
rue des Barres **79**
Belleville **162**
porte de Bercy **84**, **107**, **109**, **131**
quai de Béthune **60**
rue des Blancs-Manteaux **68**
quai de Bourbon **40**, **68**
rue Broca **113**
rue Campagne-Première **7**
Carmes (market) **141**, **145**
rue du Cherche-Midi **33**
île de la Cité **105**, **164**
gardens of the Hôtel de Cluny **129**
quai Conti **69**, **118**
porte Dauphine **180**, **182**
cour du Dragon **63**
rue de l'École-de-Médecine **72**
Eiffel Tower **14**
rue des Francs-Bourgeois **117**
rue Galande **134**
rue Geoffroy-Saint-Hilaire **69**
avenue des Gobelins **101**
avenue de la Grande-Armée **148**
rue de Grenelle **16**, **42**
rue du Grenier-sur-l'Eau **74**
rue des Haudriettes **31**
rue de l'Horloge **120**
rue de l'Hôtel de Ville **68**
porte d'Italie **24**
rue de Jarente **70**
rue Lepic **92**
quai de la Loire **135**
Louvre **16**
pont du Louvre **34**
Luxembourg gardens 3, **36**, **158**
porte Maillot **179**
place Maubert **141**, **145**
porte du Bas-Meudon **87**
cour de la Monnaie **118**
rue Montaigne **94**
rue de Montmorency **39**
Montparnasse 23, 24
rue du Montparnasse **91**
porte de Montreuil **139**
rue Mouffetard **143**
pont Neuf **65**
rue de Nevers **78**
Notre-Dame **16**
Palais-Royal **151**
rue de Palestine **162**
rue de la Parcheminerie **61**
rue du Petit-Thouars 24, **137**
boulevard Poniatowski **107**, **109**
porte du Pré-Saint-Gervais **152**
rue du Prévôt **80**
rue des Prouvaires **57**
rue Quincampoix **59**
rue Rataud **77**
cour de Rohan 14, **133**
place Saint-André-des-Arts **94**
rue Saint-André-des-Arts 14, **69**
rue Sainte-Croix-de-la-Bretonnerie **60**, **116**
canal Saint-Denis **86**

rue Saint-Jacques **32**
église Saint-Médard **153**
rue Saint-Sauveur **115**
église Saint-Séverin **28**
rue Sauval **60**, **62**
rue de Seine **142**
boulevard de Strasbourg 21
rue Suger **60**
rue Thouin **82**
quai de la Tournelle **64**, **67**
rue Transnonain 14
cité Trébert **138**
jardin des Tuileries **156**, **167**
rue des Ursins **75**
rue de Varenne **39**, **123**
rue de Vaugirard **89**, **92**
rue de la Verrerie **58**
square du Vert-Galant **105**, **164**
bassin de la Villette **135**
rue Visconti **119**
Paris de 1800 à 1900 7
Paris de nuit 23
Petits métiers 15, 22, 23, 48
Picasso, Pablo 16, 19, 188
Pougetoux, Alain 9
Proust, Marcel 23
Puyo, Constant 20
Queynet, Daniel 24
Rado, Charles 7
Raoult 48
Rapilly 48
ready-made 12, 13, 16, 188
Recherche photographique, La 9
Rembrandt 49
René-Jacques 8, 24
Renger-Patzsch, Albert 8, 16, **35**, **37**, **144**, 189
Réquillart, Bruno 8, 17, **171**, **172**, **174**, **176**, 189
Révolution surréaliste, La 7, 19, 20, 186
Reyher, Ferdinand 9
Reynaud, Françoise 9, 20
Riat, Georges 7
Rodin, Auguste 17

Ronis, Willy 24
Saint-Cloud park 14, 17, **44**, **45**, **47**, 48, **48**, 49, **49**, **50**, **51**, **52**, **53**, **54**, **55**, **169**, **170**, **171**, 186
Saint-Germain-des-Prés 1900, vu par Atget 9
Salon de l'Escalier 8
Salon indépendant de la photographie 8
Sander, August **99**
Sceaux 23, **103**, **126**, **175**, **184**, 186
Small History of Photography, A 8, 20, 21
Simon, Charles 7
Social Landscape 188
Sorbonne 188
Sougez, Emmanuel 7
Soupault, Philippe 19
Steerage 15
Steichen, Edward 21, 22
Stieglitz, Alfred 12, 15, 21, 22, 24
Stone, Sasha 20
Stotz, Gustaf 20, 21
Strand, Paul 14, 16, 22
Štyrský, Jindřich 8, 17, 20, **100**, 189
Szarkowski, John 7, 9, 21, 22, 23
Tanguy, Yves 19
Tintoretto 17
Trianon **124**
Trülzsch, Holger 14
Un siècle de photographie, de Nièpce à Man Ray 23
Utrillo, Maurice 7
Vallery-Radot, Jean 48
Vélazquez, Diego 17
Versailles 8, 14, 23, **168**, **171**, **172**, **173**, **174**, **176**, **177**, 189
Vert 23
Vlaminck, Maurice de 7
Vogue 8
Weston, Edward 8, 21
White, Minor 9, 23
Winogrand, Garry 22
Work of Atget, The 9, 21
World of Atget, The 8, 9, 20
Zadkine, Ossip 16
Zborovski 24

© 2000 Prestel Verlag, Munich · London · New York for the English-language edition
© 2000 Marval for the original edition

Front jacket: Eugène Atget, *25, rue des Francs-Bourgeois*, 1904
Back jacket: Eugène Atget, *Square du Vert-Galant, Île-de-la-Cité*, 1911

Library of Congress Card Number: 00-105944

Prestel Verlag
Mandlstrasse 26
D-80802 Munich
Germany
Tel.: (89) 38 17 09 0
Fax: (89) 38 17 09 35
www.prestel.de

4 Bloomsbury Place
London WC1A 2QA
Tel.: (020) 7323 5004
Fax: (020) 7636 8004

175 Fifth Avenue
New York
NY 10010
Tel.: (212) 995 2720
Fax: (212) 995 2733
www.prestel.com

Prestel books are available worldwide. Please contact your nearest bookseller
or any of the above addresses for information concerning your local distributor.

design
March'adour
with
Claire García-Serrano and Éric Cez
origination, printing, and binding
Musumeci
(Val d'Aoste)

Printed in Italy

English edition

editorial direction
Philippa Hurd

translation from the French
David Radzinowicz Howell

copy-editing
Lucinda Hawksley

typesetting
EDV-Fotosatz Huber / Verlagsservice G. Pfeifer, Germering

ISBN: 3-7913-2456-X